Miller & Rhoads

Legendary Santa Claus

Miller & Rhoads
Legendary Santa Claus

Written and Compiled By Kristin Terbush Thrower

ISBN: 087517115X
Library of Congress Catalog Number: 2001094236

The Dietz Press
Richmond, Virginia

Content

Dedication

This book is dedicated to all who believe in Santa Claus.

Acknowledgments

The Miller & Rhoads story would not be complete if Richmonders did not share their memories and memorabilia. Throughout the years of researching M&R and M&R Santa Claus, I have spoken to numerous people and have met many new friends. I want to thank the Richmond community for supporting this project.

This book could not have been written without the assistance of Dr. Kathryn Fuller-Seeley. Her guidance and motivation kept me going throughout the research and writing of this book. Thanks to Wayne Dementi, Dementi Studio, whose enthusiasm for this project was inspiring. Teresa Roane, Archivist, at the Valentine Richmond History Center, was instrumental in locating the M&R Records Collections and her help is appreciated. Christine S. Risatti, Executive Director of *Downtown Presents* provided valuable material on how the M&R Santa Claus arrived at *Downtown Presents*. *Downtown Presents* hard work insures that new generations of children will have the opportunity to visit the Legendary M&R Santa Claus each Christmas. A thank you goes to the staff at the *Rich-*

mond Times Dispatch Research Library.

I want to thank the members of the National Railway Historical Society, Old Dominion Chapter, in Richmond, Virginia. I have learned a lot about the Richmond, Fredericksburg and Potomac Railroad and enjoyed visiting their museum. Thank you to Richard Hogan who introduced me to this group and arranged the use of the Santa Train pictures.

I met many special Miller & Rhoads employees, who were very complimentary about working at M&R. Milton Burke's knowledge of M&R was very helpful throughout this project. I learned a great deal about M&R store windows from Allen Rhodes. Hattie Moore Garrison and Lisa McDaniel Ramos spoke eloquently about their prior jobs as Snow Queens. Seasonal M&R employee, James Hurt, had many delightful stories about what M&R was like at Christmas time. It was with great pleasure that I was able to meet and interview Eddie Weaver's daughter, Jody Weaver Wampler. John West donated *The M&R Mirror* issues for use in publication. Glenn Crone provided information on Christmas at *Downtown Presents*. Although I did not meet Charles Nuckols, he deserves a thank-you for keeping the tradition alive.

Dan Rowe has earned a special thank you, and his stories fill these pages. He brings joy and happiness to Richmonders every year. I owe a great deal to Art and Francis Hood. It was their story that provided the inspiration for this book. Art Hood was a very special man, who loved children and celebrated the Christmas holiday with them. Francis is a dear friend and holds a special place in my heart.

I would like to thank the following people for their donations to this book, including their stories and photographs. Paul and Jean Bates had wonderful stories about shopping at M&R and taking their grandchildren to see Santa Claus. Christine P. Shuart entertained me with her memories of Friday night dinners eaten in the M&R Tea Room. A delightful Saturday afternoon was spent with Debbie Kramer Broome and her mother, Patricia Fisher Sutton. Debbie's love for the M&R Santa Claus helped fill this book with beautiful photographs. Thank you to Katherine Schultheis, Martha Nelson, Margaret Comstock, Katherine Lee Queen, Louise Dickson and Ginny and Sonny McDaniel for loaning me photographs and memories.

Harry L. Seeley, Jr. and Kenny Seeley donated technical advice, which was greatly appreciated. Carolina Ipock and Charles Finley provided wonderful editing jobs. Thank you to Claire Crostic, who shared beautiful stories about M&R. Dana Bryson Greenawalt played a key role in getting this book off the ground and I will forever be grateful to her.

My parents, Tom and Judy Terbush, deserve a very big thank-you. My dad taught me to dream and to reach for those dreams. My mom was my editor, research assistant, and sounding board, all the while helping me with a newborn and a school-age child. I am grateful to Kim Terbush, who helped me locate materials and provided emotional support. Scott Terbush's positive supportive is greatly appreciated. Thank you to Hilda and Harold Thrower, who they were very patient and encouraging throughout this project.

Megan and Michael Thrower deserve their own special thank you. They are great children and I love them a lot! My husband, Pete Thrower earned the biggest thank you of all. He made all of this possible. Thank you and I love you.

Kristin Terbush Thrower

*Miller & Rhoads Christmas Catalog
Front Cover, 1958.*

Courtesy of the author

Introduction

The magic of Christmas shines through children's eyes. Several years ago I took my then four-year-old daughter Megan downtown for her first visit with the Legendary Miller & Rhoads Santa Claus. She was a lovely sight, all dressed up in her velvet holiday party dress, with white stockings and black patent leather shoes. Megan was so excited to be able to meet Santa and confide in him her Christmas wishes. She brought along her stuffed Santa Claus doll so that she could show Santa how much she loved and thought of him all through the year.

As we waited in line, Megan's eyes grew wide and she could barely stand still in her anticipation of talking with Santa. Finally, it was her turn, and she slowly approached the beautiful Snow Queen, perched on her chair on the decorated winter set. The Snow Queen conversed in low tones with Megan, asking her where she lived, her age and what toys she was going to ask for. Then Santa, in his plush suit and oh-so-real beard, seated in his large armchair, turned towards Megan and the Snow Queen, and called out Megan's name. Her face lit up at the sound of her name. She did not hesitate for an instant to move forward and sit upon the big man's knee. They had a great conversation, as Megan showed him her toy Santa and told him about her wishes. I had her picture taken with him, and then we departed for the journey back home.

The story of her visit to Santa would have ended there, except for what happened soon afterwards during our annual holiday trip to the shopping mall. Every year, we visit the mall Santa with some friends, to have a group picture taken and ride the Santa Train. This particular year, our visit to this Santa followed our trip downtown. Megan and the other children had their picture taken with the mall Santa. Then he began to ask each child what they wanted to receive for Christmas. Megan stood by quietly, listening as her friends asked for cars and dolls. I thought Megan was being very polite and patient, and I was quite proud of her. When Santa finally turned to Megan and asked, "So, little girl, and what do you want for Christmas?" she very matter-of-factly answered, with the seriousness of an adult, "I already told the Real Santa Claus what I want." I was flabbergasted. We had not discussed the earlier downtown visit with Santa, and I had never told her that some Richmonders believed the M&R Santa to be the Real Santa Claus. But Megan knew, and she had no doubt that she had already visited the Genuine Article.

I realized at that moment that the stories about the Legendary M&R Santa Claus were true. Children do not question the authenticity of this downtown Santa. They instinctively know that he is real. My daughter's experience motivated me to learn more about this celebrated figure, and so I began my investigation into the history of the M&R Santa Claus.

My research was conducted over a period of more than five years, at the Valentine Richmond History Center, the Richmond Public Library, *Richmond Times Dispatch* Archives, and during interviews with scores of former employees, customers and Santa fans who remembered standing in those long lines all during their childhood. What I found was truly fascinating! The tale of the M&R Santa Claus, however, could not be told without examining the history of the department store itself. I have taken the liberty in Chapter One of providing readers with a brief history of the Miller & Rhoads Company. I believe that in order to understand how this store's Santa Claus could become such a beloved figure in Richmond society that one must understand the relationship M&R had with the Richmond community, and with the South. So, recalling some of those waits to see Santa in his sixth floor Wonderland, please pardon the amount of detail presented in the first chapter, and enjoy this bit of nostalgia for an era gone by before you, too, get to visit with Santa. The rest of the book, Chapters Two through Seven, tells the story of the M&R Legendary Santa Claus and Christmas time at M&R. When you get to the end of the book, you may want to stick in your own photographs and souvenirs of the past visits with Santa on the blank pages, to create your own family keepsake album.

This book is my gift to Richmond and its citizens, who took it upon themselves to save such a historic figure. I hope you will enjoy reading this story as much as I have enjoyed writing it. Merry Christmas!

Richmond was the most important city in the Upper South when Miller & Rhoads opened its doors in 1885. Nowhere else in the South did a store exist of this magnitude, and for 105 years M&R was the "South's Greatest Shopping Center."

The story begins in the fall of 1885 with three young men waiting on the southbound train platform in Reading, Pennsylvania. Webster S. Rhoads, Linton O. Miller and Simon W. Gerhart quit their retail jobs and headed south to begin a new life. The men had no specific destination in mind below the Mason-Dixon Line. As the train pulled up, the three men boarded and their adventure began. It was an exciting time for the American retail world and for Richmond.[1]

All three men worked at the Dives, Pomeroy & Stewart Department Store in Reading, Pennsylvania.

Webster S. Rhoads, Sr. in a store portrait.
Photograph courtesy of Valentine Richmond History Center.

Linton O. Miller in a store portrait. c. 1910.
Dementi photograph courtesy of Valentine Richmond History Center.

Rhoads was a member of management, and he must have been aware of the changes reshaping the retail industry, including the opening of many new dry goods and department stores. The fact that all three men worked long hours in the same store meant that they had plenty of time to discuss and analyze the retail world as they knew it. The young men had saved the needed capital for a business venture, figuring that $ 3000 would be sufficient.[2]

The opening of a dry goods store in the mid-1880s was not a unique idea, for dry goods stores were then the

M&R dress goods department. 1901-1906. Photograph courtesy of Valentine Richmond History Center.

hubs of American retailing. They sold basic merchandise such as material for clothing, notions, bulk grocery items and household necessities.

The stores looked like rectangular boxes, with shelves of merchandise running down each outer wall and one row of merchandise stacked along a center aisle. Bulk merchandise storage consisted of wooden bins or big barrels where merchants spooned out staples and weighed them according to the customers' needs. Interior store decorations were nothing more than shelves stacked full of merchandise. More successful stores might have a carved wooden chicken in the window advertising eggs. Dry goods stores could not consistently stock the same merchandise due to seasonal changes and crop fluctuations. Independent dealers set their own prices and purchased locally made items. Customers and clerks bargained daily over the individual price of items. Women took the merchandise home, where they would sew the dresses and shirts and otherwise complete the item's transformation into necessary products.

Prior to department stores and set prices, the idea of "shopping" did not exist. Merchants expected purchases from customers when they entered a dry goods store and customers expected to haggle over the prices. We can imagine that timid customers dreaded the thought of having to go through a tough and probably unfair bargaining episode. The early merchants made their profits with high prices and high turnover of products.

Miller, Rhoads and Gerhart wanted to try their hand at creating their own type of store incorporating the old dry good store with the modern ideas of the department store. Following the post-Civil War Industrial Revolution, products were no longer being sold in an incomplete stage, and manufacturers needed new kinds of stores to distribute the new types of merchandise. A revolution in shopping was occurring as entrepreneurs used new ideas to challenge the old system of retailing. Dry goods stores were evolving into the new urban department stores. By 1900, the department store was firmly rooted in the social and cultural life of female shoppers.[3]

We don't know the exact reason why the three men chose Richmond as their final destination. One story said that as the men enjoyed the amenities of train travel en route to Norfolk, they discussed the advantages of Virginia's Eastern Shore. The City of Norfolk seemed ideal, due to its economic and population growth and its many ports. However, when the train pulled into Broad Street Station in Richmond, Virginia, the three men climbed out to stretch their legs. As they walked the streets, they decided that Richmond, not Norfolk, was the place to be. The three men gathered their luggage and departed the train to explore and find a location in Richmond. Another version of the story relates that their boss in Pennsylvania had told them that Richmond would be a good City in which to begin a department store, since the city was actively rebuilding from the destruction of the Civil War. Regardless of which reason was true, the fact was that the three men decided Richmond would be the home of their dry goods store.[4]

Richmond is Growing

It was an exciting time in Richmond. To the northern men, Richmond seemed to be a mecca for all types of citizens, cultures and new fascinations. Richmond has a great history. Richmond's role as the revered Capital of the Confederacy increased tourism and influenced migration to the city from other southern cities. As the former Confederate capital, Richmond was the rightful owner of the glorification and history of the Civil War. Richmonders symbolized the South's heritage within the context of the nineteenth century. The city's population had grown from 37,910 in 1860 to 63,600 in 1880. It had an excellent reputation as a center for entertainment, government and trade. It was also an important industrial and tobacco-manufacturing center. Richmond was positioned in a central location on the East Coast; it was the halfway point between the North and the South, not only geographically, but also symbolically. Richmond benefited from the northern culture of entertainment—operas, vaudeville and theater. Six railroad lines connected

Richmond to all points of America. In 1888, Richmond inaugurated the nation's first electric streetcar line. The city had finished rebuilding from the Civil War's destruction and had firmly established itself as a southern urban center. It was a perfect site to open a new store.[5]

The three men found a very small location in a building at 117 East Broad Street, eight blocks east and a world away from the older established retail section of Main Street. The one-room store measured 22x75 feet, and the name above its door read "Miller, Rhoads, & Gerhart Dry-Goods Store" (MR&G). Many Richmond skeptics doubted that the three men would open, much less succeed, due to the shop's unusual location. The men did not listen to the naysayers and they rented the small store, even though MR&G was surrounded by homes and small businesses. After securing the location, the men realized that the Virginia State Fair was going to be in town in October. The mad rush began to open the store on the same weekend that the Fair opened; they had only two months to get ready. It was exhausting work for the three men and their seven employees. Their capital of three thousand dollars was running out quickly and they could not

Opening day advertisement from the **Richmond Times Dispatch** *October 17, 1885.*

afford to purchase a plentiful supply of merchandise. The enterprising men stacked empty boxes behind the sparse array of goods in hopes of giving the appearance of a well-stocked store. The glass counters became beds to the men who worked throughout the night in order to open on October 17, 1885, just in time to greet the State Fair and the Fair's attendees.[6]

On the 17th, the men awoke to find a small group of people outside, anxious for them to open. The customers were excited about the new store because of the advertisements MR&G had placed in the local papers, inviting customers to come and see the novelty of MR&G, which included the new "one-price system" (which was very successful for the Stewart and Wanamaker's stores in New York City and Philadelphia). MR&G's founders knew that the store must be unique to be successful; they decided to label each piece of merchandise with a tag displaying a set price. They eliminated the old system of haggling. Each individual customer paid the same price for the same item. The distinctiveness of MR&G was apparent; it was the first store in Richmond to adopt the one-price system.

Miller, Rhoads & Gerhart newspaper advertisement, **Richmond Times Dispatch**, *October 25, 1885.*

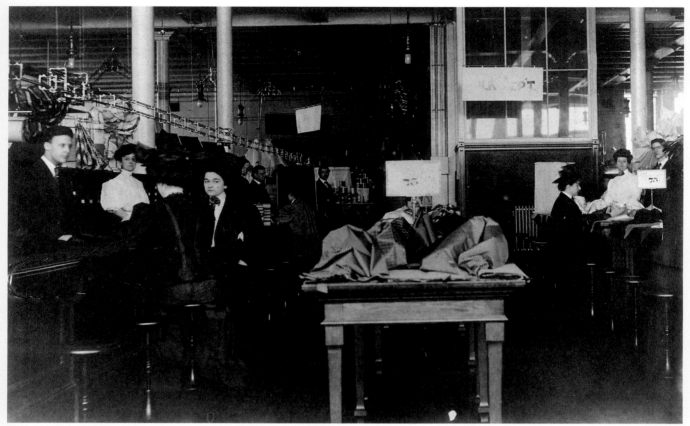

The Miller & Rhoads fabric department, 1901-1906.   Photograph courtesy of Valentine Richmond History Center.

The Idea of Service

In addition to the pricing innovation, Miller, Rhoads and Gerhart truly believed in providing higher levels of customer service. In most dry goods store, women selected items, haggled over the price and then left in a hurry. By contrast, the new department stores developed a full range of customer services, which included consumer credit, a new work force to "fawn over patrons," and the use of department store space for consumer pleasure. The attitude in the retail industry changed from "the public be damned" to "the public be served." Services provided to the customer showed the respect the shops had for the customers. By hiring ten attentive sales clerks to help its customers and providing free delivery of purchases, MR&G was on its way to providing excellent service.

The early MR&G store consisted of one long room with two aisles, one on each side of the center row of merchandise. Along the sides of the store, glass-front wooden counters provided a division between the customer and merchandise. Glass cases displayed jewelry, while bolts of material and trimmings were stored in the decorated wooden cabinetry behind the counters. The salespeople stayed behind the counters and waited for the customers to approach them. Merchandise was stored behind the counters on wall-length shelves, and store employees retrieved the wanted items and handed them to the customers. MR&G provided stools for the lady shoppers to rest on while clerks assisted them. The rear counter's primary function was for customer service. Like other modern department stores, at this counter customers could use telephones (another new

MR&G postcard, 1890s.
Courtesy of Valentine Richmond History Center.

invention), pay their charge account bills, pick up packages and return merchandise. As the store grew larger, customer services increased to include two cafes, a branch post office, a telegraph office, telephones booths, free coat and package checking booths and rest rooms. [7]

From the beginning, MR&G provided a comfortable environment for its largely female clientele through a broad range of merchandise and customer services. The merchandise that MR&G initially carried consisted of black and colored cashmere cloth, hosiery, underwear, gloves, ribbons, corsets, buttons, laces, embroideries, muslin, prints, and blankets. The merchandise clearly targeted Richmond's female population. The store demonstrated that it cared about its customers by offering the

Miller, Rhoads & Gerhart store at 509-511 East Broad Street. MR&G Staff photograph, c. 1888.

Photograph courtesy of Valentine Richmond History Center.

one-price system and accommodating clerks.[8]

The MR&G store was a huge success. In 1896, MR&G proclaimed its' success in a prominent advertisement placed in a Confederate reunion volume. MR&G also advertised in various media. At a time when postcard collecting was the fad, MR&G advertised on their own postcards. One such postcard pictured two children riding on a sled made from a spool of thread. Printed at the bottom was "MR&G one price dry goods store 117 East Broad Street." On the back was an advertisement for a nationally known brand of thread. MR&G used the growing popularity of national products to promote its own store. Another postcard linked store and community by depicting the historical sights of Richmond next to the M&R store.[9]

Growing with the Times

The years between 1888 and 1919 saw the store's expansion and evolution into a full-fledged department store. Within three short years, the store expanded from its original depth of 75 feet to 130 feet. Founder Simon Gerhart ventured to Lynchburg, Virginia, in 1888, to open a MR&G branch at 820 Main Street. Ten years later in 1898, Gerhart split off from the group on friendly terms and exchanged all his stock in the Richmond MR&G for all the stock of the Lynchburg store. Rhoads and Miller renamed their Richmond store Miller & Rhoads, and in 1906, the store became incorporated. By 1909, M&R was the largest department store in Richmond.[10]

In early July 1888, Rhoads sent a letter to William Grant Swartz offering him a position in management as the floor manager in the Richmond store. Swartz's responsibilities would be to make sure that "every customer received the proper attention and that salespeople performed their part in a satisfactory manner." Rhoads had served as floor manager at Miller & Rhoads but the store's growth had increased his office duties; he therefore had less time to devote to hands-on store management. The manager offer included two yearly leaves of absences for a week, or ten days, and a yearly salary of one thousand dollars. Swartz's reply posed questions regarding the position and Richmond's economic health. Rhoads' last letter stressed the conservative nature of Richmond society, which appealed to him. As a northerner, Rhoads admitted that he would live in no place other than Richmond. Swartz did not accept the Richmond store position, but instead, M&R and Swartz formed a partnership and in 1888 Swartz opened a M&R branch in Norfolk, Virginia.

First floor at Christmas time. 1940-1950.　　　　　　　　　　Photograph courtesy of Dementi Studio.

The association between stores continued until 1927 when Swartz purchased the Norfolk store's stocks and became an independent owner.[11]

Rhoads' letters to Swartz revealed how important the customer was to the store. The manager's duties pertained to the shoppers' experience in the store, making sure the employees treated them with respect and devoted their full attention to them. The men considered the customer their number one priority and the best advertising their store could have.

In 1888, M&R moved to a larger location at 500-511 East Broad Street. Rhoads and Miller continued to expand, and in 1901, the two-story section at 509 East Broad Street grew by two more floors. The small, canopy-covered windows were transformed into a wall of plate

Elevator Porters, First Floor elevators, Grace Street Side. c. 1935.

Photograph courtesy of the author.

glass a city block long that displayed the world of merchandise available inside. By 1919, M&R had acquired the remaining land on Grace Street between 5th and 6th Streets to make the store an entire block wide.[12]

The year 1917 was a sad one for the young M&R store. Linton O. Miller died on April 26, 1917 at the age of 77. The employees eulogized Miller through many articles, prayers and condolences published in the M&R employee magazine, the *Mirror*. Employees missed Miller's presence. Sorrow extended into the Richmond community, as it lost one of its civic leaders. Douglas S. Freeman wrote a memorial editorial on Mr. Miller in the *Richmond Times Dispatch*. Mr. Miller, after all, was a true gentleman; he forever examined new ideas with full attention to details. Miller was an honest, hardworking man, a Horatio Alger hero in Richmond; he exemplified the perfect manager. Having started as a clerk and later becoming an owner, he saw the business from both sides. Miller understood how hard the sales clerk's job was and supported the store's employees psychologically with respect and materially with employee benefits.[13]

By 1920, the store was firmly established as a high quality depart-

First floor at Christmas time. 1940-1950. Photograph courtesy of Dementi Studio.

ment store. The look and feel of M&R expressed elegance. Uniformed salespeople waited behind the glass-fronted counters, where the customer explored an expansive array of merchandise enclosed in cases made of American walnut. Fine leather gloves, linen handkerchiefs and delicate jewelry filled the cases. If the customer looked around, she would find the walls also lined with American walnut. She chose from six passenger elevators with attendants to whisk her to the upper floors. She could also ride an escalator surrounded by mirrored walls and platforms decorated with displays of the exquisite merchandise for sale.[14]

The customer found telephone booths for local and long distance calls. M&R's services included lost-and-found desks; stamps and telegraph desks, wrapping desks (for shipping and mailing), an exchange desk and information bureaus. M&R's services extended to providing the public with time schedules for trains and buses, movies and plays. The store posted want ads from Richmond newspapers for the convenience of the customer. Large public restrooms were located on all floors. The second and fifth floor restrooms were for customers only. The second floor restroom provided reading and writing facilities for more than one hundred ladies.

M&R gathered merchandise from around the world: Turkish rugs, Venetian glassware, handmade fine linens from Italy, chinaware and jewelry from Austria, Japanese silk robes and the finest decorative gifts from France. M&R buyer, Arthur W. Bates, wrote from France, "I am over here collecting the new things for the shopping center."[15]

In 1935, M&R celebrated its 50th anniversary with a Golden Jubilee celebration. It was an exciting time at the store. Although the Great Depression raged on, M&R continued to enjoy years of profit and prosperity. The 50-year anniversary was a proud moment. Its many years of service reaffirmed that the store had firmly established itself within the Richmond community.[16]

The 1940s were a turning point in M&R's history, with Rhoads, Sr.'s passing and Rhoads, Jr.'s absence during mili-

M&R Christmas Catalog Front Cover, c. 1956.
Courtesy of the author.

tary service. For the first time, a founder or family member did not run M&R. Absalom B. Laughon became president of M&R in 1942. Laughon had begun working at M&R in 1906, shortly after the Company incorporated. His previous position at M&R was vice president and general manager. He remained President until his death in June 1944. Upon Laughon's death, Frank T. Bates, store Junior. vice president and secretary-treasurer, became the new president. Mr. Bates was the last of the older generation of officers.[17]

Branching Out

Throughout the 1950s and 1960s, M&R expanded its operations into smaller cities. M&R acquired the Stevens Shepherd chain in 1947 (with stores in Charlottesville, Norfolk and Chapel Hill, North Carolina) and J.R. Millner in 1957 (Lynchburg). From 1949 to 1953, the Stevens Shepherd chain showed a loss, and the stores were a drain on the M&R Corporation; M&R closed the stores or converted them into M&R satellite branches. The merger with J.R. Millner was seen as beneficiary to M&R, since the stockholders did not need to issue any additional preferred stock, and this increased M&R's net worth. This store

M&R, the newly expanded Richmond store. c. 1950.
Photograph courtesy of Dementi Studio.

In 1960, M&R celebrated their 75th anniversary with a Diamond Jubilee. Throughout the first floor, the Christmas decorations were scenes from 1885.
Photograph courtesy of Dementi Studio.

was Lynchburg's largest department store, and in 1958, its name was changed to M&R. The store leased half the block across the street to create a parking lot for 140 cars.[18]

M&R's Charlottesville location opened on August 16, 1956, at the northwest corner of Main and East 4th street. The store had a total of 45,000 square feet of floor space. It emphasized ready-to-wear clothes for women and children. The store also had a Tea Room that Santa visited during Christmas time.[19]

The Roanoke store was opened on September 4, 1957. The store was at the southeast corner of Campbell Avenue and 1st Street. The modern building had 126,000 square feet of space, including six floors and a basement. The Roanoke store carried a full line of merchandise and re-

Christmas decorations, c. 1960.
Photograph courtesy of Dementi Studio.

sembled the Richmond store. Santa didn't visit this store.[20]

In 1953, M&R's downtown Richmond store began expanding on 5th and Broad Streets. M&R built a new store for F.W. Woolworth, and when it was completed, M&R leased the 4th floor and 33 feet on Broad Street of the first and second floor, expanding the pre-existing store. The completed Richmond downtown store now contained over 300,000 square feet.[21]

In 1959, plans were made to open the first Richmond suburban branch of M&R, located at the new Willow Lawn Shopping Center. From 1961 to 1966, M&R opened nine other branch stores across Virginia. These stores ranged in size from 16,000 to 83,000 square feet. But the 1960s were an era of mergers and corporate consolidations among the department stores seeking to maintain their position in a changing market. In

Christmas decorations, c. 1960.
Photograph courtesy of Dementi Studio.

1967, the Julius Garfinckel Company acquired M&R. Then in 1981, M&R was acquired once more, this time by Allied, a national holding company. In 1987, the store's top management decided to buy back the store, and once again it was locally owned and managed.[22]

What enabled the store to succeed throughout the years was the direct connection it forged with the community. From the beginning, M&R treated the Richmond community with respect. M&R of Richmond was no different from the increasingly opulent northern department stores, such as Wanamaker's and Macy's, in providing customer services. In 1910, M&R had offered charge plates and free home delivery service for items customers purchased. M&R first delivered purchases in horse-drawn delivery carriages, which were operated from their horse stable that included twelve wagons and twenty-four horses. Between 1910 and World

Christmas decorations, c. 1960.   Photograph courtesy of Dementi Studio.

War I, M&R phased out the carriages and replaced them with gasoline-powered delivery trucks. Longtime M&R employee, Robert Price, however, still preferred the horse carriages to the gasoline trucks, stating that they could carry more merchandise. One did not have to worry about parking, setting the brake, or on what side of the road one drove.[23]

The Personal Touch

For a great business to succeed it must have great salespeople. The M&R employee was the store's most important customer service tool. The founders established an idea from day one that each customer was to be treated as an invited guest in the store. M&R's store philosophy was simply put, "Between the patrons and the management there is more to be desired than mere selling: an abiding friendship is involved far

Christmas decorations, c. 1960.   Photograph courtesy of Dementi Studio.

above profit." This was even written on M&R shopping bags. M&R trained its employees to believe this motto. M&R employees waited on their customers; sometimes the customer never touched the merchandise until it was delivered to her home.[24]

Webster Rhoads was a common sight on the selling floors as he greeted both employees and customers. Rhoads and Miller believed well-behaved employees produced customers loyal to the store. The *M&R Rules and Regulations for the Guidance of Employees* handbooks, published annually between 1888 and 1917, laid out strict expectations concerning personal appearance, behavior and store rules. M&R believed that service was vital to the store's image. Therefore, since the employees had daily contact with the customers, the employees' behavior and appearance were very important. Manuals continually stressed the store policy

Christmas decorations, c. 1960.   Photograph courtesy of Dementi Studio.

that the employees' number one responsibility was the customer. *M&R's Store System and General Store Rules Book* in 1927 portrayed the atmosphere of the store as a "refined home." "In your dress, your manner of speech, and in your general attitude try to give this impression...Act as if you were in a refined home and the customers were your guests."[25] Emion Smith wrote in a letter to all sales managers,

> "M&R waits patiently for people to arrive, to give him breath, life and reason for being. We are M&R, each and every one of us. Together we give our store its name and character in the community; each time we come in contact with a customer, we are speaking not only for ourselves."[26]

M&R's concern for the community went beyond the inside of the store. During World War II, the store grew a victory garden and sold war bonds. M&R employees were quite proud of their victory garden, located at the corner of Hamilton and Broad Streets. Store employees grew English peas, radishes, onions, mustard greens, spinach, Swiss chard, squash, corn, tomatoes, snaps, butter beans and white squash. The Methodist orphanage received the bountiful harvest. M&R began selling war bonds on September 9, 1941 to both its employees and the public. To encourage selling, M&R offered prizes to the employees who sold the most. The prize for class A and B employees was a fifty-dollar bond while the top African American employee received a twenty-five-dollar bond. M&R had placed a quota on the store to sell $ 350,000 worth of bonds; they even held a special employee-buying day on September 25th, and the store surpassed its quota. After we officially entered the war, as Americans learned how to watch the skies for enemy airplanes, M&R published pamphlets that provided detailed instructions for what the public should do during air raids and described different types of bombs. The store practiced air raid drills and concluded the drills with group singing of "God Bless America," "Smiles," "Onward Christian Soldiers" and "Pack Up Your Troubles."[27]

It was these examples of community pride, excellent service and respect that made M&R into a beloved institution in Richmond. M&R's first floor clock became a Richmond landmark, a well-known rendezvous where customers or employees regularly met and then ventured into the store. "Meet me under the clock," needed no further explanation for thousands of Richmonders and Virginians. The ornate timepiece with four separate clock faces was located on the first floor. The M&R information desk was located under the clock. Mrs. Kitty Duke, an M&R employee who staffed the Information Desk, recalled that Richmonders felt connected to her. Many shoppers considered Mrs. Duke a part of their extended family. Her desk was included in visits to the store, where shoppers talked about their families, introduced the new babies and sometimes gave her small gifts or flowers. Not only did the information desk provide a list of store officials, list of wedding symbols, city directory, and list of store employees who spoke foreign languages, but its staff also could direct customers to the bulletin boards that posted bus schedules.

M&R first floor clock.
Photograph taken at the Valentine Richmond
History Center by the author.

In 1982, when M&R retired the information desk clerk, protest letters and phone calls were instrumental in M&R rehiring the clerk! F. Winfrey Carter, a retired M&R employee, wrote to the *Richmond News Leader*, "Mrs. Kitty Duke was not only an institution but also a living monument. She was a truly wonderful lady who helped countless thousands of people…The clock that Mrs. Duke sat under was as popular as Big Ben in London."[28]

So, it is no surprise that when the "Real" Santa Claus first visited M&R in 1936, he would become part of Richmond's history. In 1942, Santa sealed his position in families' traditions and as a Richmond institution, when he singled out Richmond as his permanent residence from Thanksgiving to Christmas Eve.

M&R Christmas Catalog Front Cover, 1959.

Courtesy of the author.

Chapter Two

Christmas at Miller & Rhoads

By the 1930s, M&R symbolized Richmond culture and society; M&R stood for strong character, ethics and pride. It was then that M&R established the tradition of the Legendary M&R Santa Claus. M&R housed the "Real" Legendary Santa every year, along with Snow Queens,

"Twas the Night Before Christmas." 1940-1950.
Photograph courtesy of Dementi Studio.

elves, a magic chimney and Eddie Weaver on the piano and organ. M&R *was* Christmas to people of all ages. In 1936, the Real Santa first visited the M&R store, and visited annually and then in 1942, he decided to stay.

The first image of Santa Claus in America appeared in 1809 in New York City; following this Santa, many different images and personalities emerged, but it was Clement Clark Moore's Santa character that Americans fell in love with and most imagined Santa being like. The American Santa Claus first appeared in 1823 in the story by Professor Clement Clark Moore, *'Twas the Night Before Christmas*. Thomas Nast's drawings for *Harper's Weekly Magazine* from 1863 to 1886 created the modern image of Santa that complemented Moore's Santa Claus. Nast's 1881 *Harper's Weekly* Santa, with round cheeks, white hair and beard, smoking a pipe and wearing a furry red coat became America's favorite holiday symbol.[29]

By the late 1800s, the bigger department stores in New York City, Chicago and Philadelphia, had created the fantasy world of visiting Santa. All of the wonder of Christmas was seen displayed in the street-level store windows. In 1883, decorative windows at Macy's displayed dolls and mechanical toys with steam-powered, moving figures. Gimbels, in Philadelphia, sponsored the first Thanksgiving holiday parade that included Santa in 1920. Hudson's, in Detroit, and the New York Macy's soon had their own holiday Santa parades. In 1939, Rudolph the Red Nose Reindeer was born.[30]

In Richmond, M&R also celebrated Christmas through its beautifully decorated Christmas windows-some fifty display sections that sur-

M&R behind the scenes. M&R had many departments that operated outside of the public view, such as the window and display departments. Here, M&R employees are working with wood to create an interior or window display. 1940-1960.   Photograph courtesy of Dementi Studio.

rounded the store on Broad Street, Grace Street, 5th Street and 6th Street. M&R's Christmas windows equaled those of the northern department stores. M&R hired designer R. Addison Lewis on October 18, 1895. Lewis, an M&R employee for fifty-two years, was instrumental in the design of the windows and helped establish the artistic community in Richmond.[31]

The window display department began the Christmas window preparation at least six months in advance. M&R carpenters, decorators, electricians, artists, seamstresses and sign writers worked hard to plan and

The card in the window reads, "It's Christmas time at Miller & Rhoads. Give them a gift for their home. Make it something lovely…something useful." Christmas window, 1950-1960.

Photograph courtesy of Dementi Studio.

execute the final designs into beautifully artistic windows. The few items that M&R could not easily reproduce were rented or purchased. For the most part, however, M&R designed and built the windows from beginning to end. During the last week of November, the Christmas windows were put in place and of course the windows were shielded from public view by paper, so the display team could work without the prying eyes of passersby. The secrecy also added to the sense of anticipation! The window display department began working at 7 a.m. and worked until noon or longer setting up the design.

The M&R windows were as popular as any Christmas windows in

"The Nativity Window," M&R Christmas, 1950-1960. Photograph courtesy of Dementi Studio.

New York City. A Christmas trip downtown was a must for many families. Crowds three to four people deep filled the sidewalks as people admired the spectacularly decorated windows, and the store dazzled the masses with Christmas scenes and beautiful merchandise. Nighttime was especially popular since M&R kept the windows lit and the animations on way into the night.[32]

Different Weeks, Different Themes

The M&R windows expressed both the religious and commercial sides of Christmas. Beginning the day after Thanksgiving, the Grace Street windows were re-decorated weekly in four different themes. The first week, the displays began the Christmas theme with a showcase of beauty products. Each window displayed merchandise from different cosmetic companies. The second week a new display exhibited a wide range of gift ideas for mothers, such as fine china, sterling silver place settings, perfumes, scarves, sweaters and purses. Women envisioned themselves in the beautifully displayed clothing worn so gracefully by the mannequins. It was easy to dream of serving a Christmas dinner with the fine china and sterling silverware in the next window. The following week, the decorated Grace Street windows exhibited items from the furniture department.[33]

"Peace on Earth," M&R Christmas window, 1950-1960.
Photograph courtesy of Dementi Studio.

The final Christmas holiday week was the most important with regards to the spirit of Christmas. The week before Christmas, the Grace Street windows were decorated to honor the birth of Christ. The Grace Street windows taught children the Christmas story as clearly as a Sunday school lesson. Children and adults would often "read" the window story that began at the

"Toys," M&R Christmas window, c. 1950.
Photograph courtesy of Valentine Richmond History Center.

corner of Grace and 5th and continued east towards the corner of Grace and 6th Street.

M&R artists painted the background panels to set the stage for the papier-mâché figurines. Each window resembled a book page and detailed a certain part of the religious story, including the nativity scene, with all the animals, wise men and the manger.

The nativity scene alternated years with the image of the Madonna. The Madonna was displayed in one of two ways. The window display artists painted copies of famous artistic renderings of the Madonna and Child. In this instance, the oil paintings were the only objects in the windows. M&R's Grace Street windows strove to present the real spirit and meaning of Christmas. The Madonna and Child were sometimes

The train window that showed the Virginia state landscape. The train runs from Richmond to Charlottesville to Roanoke. M&R had a store in each one of these cities. 1950-1096.

Dementi photograph courtesy of Allen Rhodes.

displayed in the form of papier-mâché figurines. Each window showed Mary and the Baby Jesus in a different pose. Again, this image was the sole feature of the window.

The Grace Street religious windows were quite popular, yet the windows that entertained children were just as popular. Here children shopped the "window catalogs" and dreamed of all the goodies that might materialize under their trees on Christmas morning.

Little girls were drawn to the doll windows. Any doll imaginable, from Howdy Doody to the classic baby doll, was showcased along with as many as 30 other dolls. Little girls dreamed of owning such fine dolls. Accessories were also displayed, such as carriages and doll clothes. Naturally the M&R toy department had all the dolls and a beautiful collec-

Richmond Train Window. M&R had different train windows throughout the years. All train windows focused on towns where M&R had a store. This photograph shows Richmond's downtown. c. 1950.

Photograph courtesy of Dementi Studio.

tion of Madame Alexander dolls available for sale.

One of the most well known windows was the train window. At the corner of 5th and Grace Streets, directly across from the Loews Theater, this fascinated many young boys and filled their Santa wish lists. Little noses and sticky hands pressed up against the windows, as children watched the trains move around the tracks.

The train exhibit contained three train tracks that ran three different trains. The train closest to the glass window was the largest, while the train farthest away was the smallest, creating the visual effect of space.[34]

The scenery of the train route changed every couple of years. But the scenery always included the cities or towns in which M&R had a store. Some years the scenery emphasized the countryside from Richmond to

M&R employee, Allen Rhodes, began working in the Window Display department in 1951. Rhodes was responsible for painting the wall murals in the Tea Room. He also worked on the window decorations. Rhodes was lucky enough to work on the famous Christmas Train window. Rhodes positioned the three trains to cross at the same time and then took this picture. c. 1950.

Photograph courtesy of Allen Rhodes.

Closer view of the three-train crossing, c. 1950.   Photograph courtesy of Allen Rhodes.

Another view of the Richmond Train Window. Here you see downtown to Dogwood Dell. c. 1950.

Photograph courtesy of Dementi Studio.

Roanoke, and showed Charlottesville along the route. A M&R sign pointed to the store's location. Other train exhibits emphasized the cities of Charlottesville, Roanoke and Richmond and highlighted their primary buildings.

The most popular train window was the window that concentrated on the City of Richmond. The window display artists were able to build the famous Richmond City three-train crossing. Children and parents stood for hours, waiting to see if the three trains would cross the bridges all at the same time.

M&R's train windows held a special position in the hearts of many young boys. Typically, the toy trains began to run one hour before the store opened and chugged along until 9 pm. In the early 1960s, the last

The "Enchanted Forest." c. 1964.

Photograph courtesy of Dementi Studio.

of the annual train windows was removed; slot cars had come into fashion and trains had lost their appeal. Although, the M&R train window continued to make an appearance every few years at Christmas time.

The children's windows were not always aimed at either just boys or girls. In 1964 the "Enchanted Forest" displayed children bringing Christmas to the forest animals. Even here in the secular celebration of Christmas, the true meaning was evident, as children presented gifts to the woodland creatures. Other than the thirty-two animated figures, the M&R staff created the rest of the display.[35]

One year, M&R decorated the children's windows in a fairy tale theme. Mother Goose, Jack and Jill and Cinderella entertained and fascinated the children. Each window was framed by a book page and had little children dressed in nightclothes who looked in at the "picture." Once

*"Mother Goose." M&R
Christmas window, c. 1948.*
Photograph courtesy of Valentine
Richmond History Center.

"Jack and Jill." M&R Christmas window, c. 1948.
Photograph courtesy of Valentine Richmond History Center.

"The Night Before Christmas." M&R Christmas window, c. 1950.

Photograph courtesy of Valentine Richmond History Center.

again, the window display department put on a spectacular show with beautiful costumes and scenery.

"The Night Before Christmas" was also a very special window. The story was placed in a shadow box with the outside frame covered in Christmas decorations. The scene inside the shadow box displayed Santa placing presents under the tree.

The Stag Shop

Shopping was a central part of the Christmas season, but not everyone approached the task with glee. M&R made shopping easier for the male customer with the first floor Stag Shop. Only male customers were allowed to pass through the entrance guarded by two Stag heads. This shop was almost concealed from the rest of the first floor and was located at the isolated corner of the building on the 6th and Broad Street side. The Stag Shop was quiet, compared to the outside hustle and bustle. The shop was created to help shopping-challenged men select appropriate gifts. Gentlemen were treated to a quiet retreat that eased their shopping fears as attentive store clerks helped them fulfill their wives' and girlfriends' Christmas wish lists. Men were shown a wide assortment of gifts from all floors and departments. If they had any hesitation about a gift, a store model was available to display it for him. She modeled everything from scarves to lingerie. The Stag Shop also offered a complete selection of merchandise for men, from shoes to furnishings. This allowed men to accomplish a one-stop shopping trip. Once he selected his purchases, the sales clerk wrapped and delivered the presents to the address given by the customer, which saved him the frustration of wrapping oddly-shaped gifts. Again, we can see the efforts of M&R to make it easy and enjoyable to shop-even for men.[36]

"Entrance to Stag Shop. A Christmas Shop for Men Only." 1940-1950.
Photograph courtesy of Valentine Richmond History Center.

Christmas Gifts, 1950-1960.   Photograph courtesy of Valentine Richmond History Center.

Santa Claus arrives in Richmond. c. 1950.
From the collection of Frances & Art Hood.

Chapter Three

Arrival of Santa Claus

*L*egend has it that in 1935, around the time of the Golden Jubilee, M&R received a visit from a very distinguished man. This man, of course, was Santa Claus. Santa Claus had heard marvelous things about the city of Richmond, M&R and the city's children; therefore, he decided to visit. At that time, Santa was searching for a temporary home between Thanksgiving and Christmas Eve. Santa liked to visit with children during the holidays. He also wanted to pass on the spirit of Christmas, which was love and giving to others.[37]

M&R set up a visiting place in the toy department, which was a logical place for Santa to meet all the children. Besides, the toy department was Santa's favorite part of the store. Many children wondered how Santa took time away from the "true" North Pole to operate out of Richmond. Santa explained that he continued to conduct Christmas business everywhere, because of the "Santa helpers" that existed in Richmond and all over the world.

M&R held coloring contests for the children, which encouraged their creativity, but more importantly, encouraged their involvement with the store to persuade Santa to reside in Richmond. Word spread quickly that the <u>Real</u> Santa Claus had arrived at M&R, and by the late 1930's, families traveled from far away (as far north as New Jersey), to visit with Santa at M&R. Children stood in line for hours to meet with him and sit on his knee. Santa's loving manner and personal attention to each child convinced even the most skeptical non-believers that this was the true Santa.[38]

After their visit with Santa, Mr. Writtonmaker, a M&R seasonal employee, drew sketches of the well-dressed children. The affordable price of one dollar and fifty cents made the drawings an ideal present for grandparents, since the grandchildren were dressed in their best clothes and still had big smiles on their faces from their visit with Santa.

Santa continued his annual visit to M&R and in 1942, Richmond and M&R received the very best Christmas gift. Santa Claus decided that Richmond, Virginia, would be his permanent home from Thanksgiving to Christmas Eve. Children saw the Real Santa only in Richmond. Santa's decision to reside in Richmond during the holidays established a family tradition for generations to come. In 1942 alone, the Legendary Santa saw an estimated 15,000 children.[39]

Santa's great friend, Bill Strothers, was instrumental in Santa's decision to live here. In 1942, Mrs. Strothers read a classified advertisement that sounded perfect for her husband, Bill Strothers. The Strothers lived in

M&R Advertisement in **Richmond News Leader**, *December 7, 1934.*

"Visiting with Santa Claus." c. 1940.   Photograph courtesy of Valentine Richmond History Center.

Petersburg, Virginia, and had attempted to manage a small inn. They needed some additional income. The M&R classified advertisement announced that the store was searching for an assistant for Santa during the holiday season. Mrs. Strothers thought her husband was right for the job, due to his strong beliefs about Santa and Christmas. [40]

Bill Strothers was an interesting man. He was familiar with the public arena. His public career started before World War I, when he worked as a stuntman named "The Human Fly." He traveled around the country, performing stunts and climbing tall buildings. His daring escapades landed him in Hollywood, where he found employment as a stuntman and actor. He appeared with Harold Lloyd in the movie *Safety Last*. Strothers remained a stunt double until shortly after he was married.

He retired from stunt work at the age of thirty and then toured in vaudeville with a performing dog, Husky. At Christmas time, Strothers and Husky visited sick children. Then in 1931, the Strothers returned to the East coast and opened an inn in Petersburg.

In 1942, Strothers responded to the M&R classified and described his idea for building a "Santa Wonderland" to M&R's management and Santa. Strothers, like Santa, believed that the true Santa communicated to children the spirit of Christmas, which was the simple and profound belief in the need for rising above selfishness by thinking of others.

Following conversations with Strothers and the M&R management, Santa Claus made his decision to reside in Richmond. Santa Claus had used the toy department for his visits with children, but now that his decision to settle at the store permanently had been reached, M&R turned to a store carpenter, Arthur "Art" G. Hood, to build a new Santa Land. This Santa Land was the appropriate place for Santa's needs.

The Santa Set

The Old Dominion Room on the store's seventh floor was magically transformed into Santa Land the day after Thanksgiving, 1942. The transformation was so complete that even the room's atmosphere felt different.

The Old Dominion Room seemed "colder" due to the hazy blue-sky effect created on the room's ceiling. The lighting effect was accomplished by painting the ceiling a light blue and focusing soft white lights on it from the alcove. The air felt chilly, just like the air at the North Pole. In addition to the lights, the alcove held Christmas decorations. Angels hung from the sky, suspended in white clouds, which glittered like diamonds.

The Santa Wonderland Set, 1996.   Courtesy of the author.

The clouds were made of angel hair, a fine glass spun to look ethereal.[41]

The chimney was a very important part of the living room, because Santa began each day there. It was rumored that right above the chimney, somewhere in the store, was where Santa slept. M&R's roof was the reindeers' landing strip. Here they took off and landed each year. To the right of the chimney sat the focal point of the room, Santa's chair. It was here that Santa called children by name and heard their utmost desires and wishes. A Christmas tree stood behind Santa and was decorated with simple ornaments that matched the beautiful evergreen wreath.

Just beyond the tree sat the Snow Queen, who wore an exquisite floor-length dress, white as snow, made of satin and lace. Little girls might imagine wearing such a dress on their wedding day. The rhinestones on

Snow Queen Hattie Moore Garrison.
Photograph courtesy of
Hattie Moore Garrison.

Snow Queen Lisa McDaniel Ramos.
Photograph courtesy of
Lisa McDaniel Ramos.

the Snow Queen's tiara sparkled in the light. Her soft voice and delicate manner gave her the ability to calm anxious children. The beautiful Snow Queen assisted by preparing the children for their special visit with Santa Claus. For some children the visit overwhelmed and terrified them. The Snow Queen reassured the child that Santa was a loving man and wanted children to be happy. The Snow Queen loved being a special helper to Santa and saw that Christmas was magical in the eyes of a child.[42]

An elf sat to Santa's left. The elf wore a red and green suit, with very pointy shoes and a matching pointy hat. The elf made sure that Santa's supply bucket of small goodies, which he handed out to all the children, was always full. A white door to the left of the chimney was where the Snow Queen and elf entered the room.

Thanks to Strothers, Hood and other M&R employees, Santa's home away from home was complete. This room housed Santa's throne where he showered love on all his visitors.

After Santa decided to reside permanently in Richmond during the holidays, he changed one part of the M&R Christmas celebration. For a time Felix the Clown and his pet pig, Amelia, visited children and celebrated Christmas with Santa at M&R. Felix Adler was the King of Clowns from the Ringling Brothers and Barnum and Bailey Circus. He entertained children in the Santa Land line and also in the Tea Room.

Felix the Clown's trick was his pet pig, Amelia. Wherever Felix walked, Amelia followed him. Felix allowed children to fed Amelia. Felix's nose lit up, and he had a big behind that was created with a bustle. As Amelia entertained the children, Felix made flowers pop out of a hat. At the end of his show, Felix raised his left pant leg and "read" the alarm clock there. No matter what time it was, Felix always said it was quarter to, and it was time to go.[43]

Felix and Amelia were popular with the children, but they did not completely fit with the ideas Santa and M&R had of what the Christmas season truly meant. The clown was purely entertainment, and although parts of Christmas were also considered entertainment, Christmas at M&R stressed the holiday season as a time for unconditional giving and love. Felix the Clown moved on in the 1950s.

Felix the Clown, **The M&R Mirror**, *1953.*
Photograph courtesy of Frances and Art Hood.

Santa Claus. 1950-1960.   Photograph courtesy of Dementi Studio.

Chapter Four

Going to see Santa

The Big Event was quite important to Richmonders and especially to children. Santa's arrival at M&R marked the countdown to Christmas and the beginning of the Christmas shopping season. Only the M&R Santa magically appeared by sliding down the chimney. After all, he was the Real Santa Claus!

We can imagine that on their "appointed day" sometime between Thanksgiving and Christmas Eve, children awoke early, filled with excitement. While some children rushed through their early morning routines and went to school, other children's mornings were quite different. They were going to visit Santa Claus instead of going to school. It is said that a visit to the M&R Santa Claus and illness were the only valid reasons to miss school in early December. "Time to get up," mothers said. Children were barely able to eat their breakfasts as they thought of the adventures that lay ahead of them. Mothers rushed about the house filling strollers and goodie bags. They dressed their children in their special Sunday clothes, scrubbed their children's faces and hands and combed their hair. You had to look your best to see Santa!

Some parents picked their children up early from school in order to return home to change into their Christmas outfits. Parents hoped to beat the rest of the Santa crowd to M&R. On weekends during the holiday season, the store was crowded, and the lines were long.

A trip downtown for any child was a visit full of wonder, because it was where Dad worked and Mother shopped. Children didn't often accompany their mothers for downtown shopping, so any journey into the city was a treat.

All dressed and clean, excited children and mothers headed to the family car. The event was so special that some fathers took the day off from work and either drove the family to M&R or met them there. The excursion downtown could be a whole day affair.

Car horns, blaring sirens, and other urban noises filled the air and added to the exhilaration of the trip. The M&R building seemed so tall and majestic. [All seven stories of the building celebrated with decorations of the Christmas season.] Children looked at the M&R rooftop and hoped to see a reindeer or two.

Whether having traveled ten minutes or twelve hours, the destination was the same-Miller & Rhoads. On the top floor, Santa Claus waited. Yes, Richmond, there was a Santa Claus, and he lived at M&R!

The first magical day of Santa's annual visit was the day after Thanksgiving. Santa saw the first child at 9:30 a.m. Yet, on this day each year, crowds lined up as early as 7:00 a.m. These families wanted to be sure to witness the historic event, when Santa came down the chimney. The crowd would arrive so early that they had to wait outside the store until

The Christmas crowd in the Old Dominion Room waiting to see Santa Claus. In the distance you can see Santa holding a young child. 1950-1960.   Photograph courtesy of Dementi Studio.

M&R's doors opened. M&R opened early and allowed the crowd to line up inside the store. The customers were not allowed to shop; they went straight to the elevator that took them up to Santa Land. All store elevators went to the seventh floor, but one special elevator, "Santa Land Express," went only to the seventh floor with no stops. The Old Dominion Room soon filled up, and the long lines of parents and children snaked in a circle around the escalators and all the way back to the elevators.

Waiting for Santa

The crowds that had lined up at seven a.m. still had to wait until Santa arrived at 9:30 a.m. Depending on the children's place in line, they might wait an additional sixty to ninety minutes to visit with him. Some-

This scene decorated a wall in the Old Dominion Room. 1950-1960.   Photograph courtesy of Dementi Studio.

times it was not uncommon for parents and children to wait two hours or more to visit with Santa. Although this seemed like a long wait, just for a visit with Santa, true believers felt that the long line was part of the trip. Parents brought snacks, books and small toys to entertain their children. A bathroom located in the Old Dominion room was a convenient break.

M&R's female employees monitored the long lines, wearing a special suit that identified their job. Rarely was there any disorderly conduct by any of the parents or children, since everybody knew that Santa was watching and saw if children were naughty or nice. Firemen also supervised the audience in the overcrowded Old Dominion Room.

Santa lines were notoriously long. In the store's later years, little scenes

The seating area in the Old Dominion Room. 1950-1960.   Photograph courtesy of Valentine Richmond History Center.

along the line route entertained the youngsters. But in the early years of Santa, there was little to entertain the children or parents, and they struck up conversations with the people around them. By the time it was the children's turn to sit on Santa's lap, the surrounding crowd felt like family. This was true for the families who saw Santa every year on the same day of the season, such as the day after Thanksgiving or Christmas Eve. Year after year, families recognized other families and continued their conversations from where they left had off from the year before. It was rare to stand in the Santa line without recognizing someone. Children believed that the waiting line equalized all children in the eyes of Santa, because everybody stood in line, regardless of their celebrity status or

Santa's legs in the chimney. c. 1980.

Photograph courtesy of Debbie Kramer Broome.

the station of their parents. Everybody mingled and talked as they waited in line. The only children who did not stand in line were those who were physically incapable. In the Santa line, everybody was a friend.[44]

Once the family was inside Santa Land, they heard what Santa told the children. Santa spoke into a microphone in his left hand. When Santa asked the child a question, he placed the microphone at the child's mouth. This ensured that parents heard the sweet conversations.

Grandparents and store employees filled the front seating area to witness the opening day of the Christmas season. This was a favorite pastime for many Richmonders, who sat in Santa Land and just watched the pleasurable visits between children and Santa.

As the line filled up, tension and excitement filled the air. "Will he remember me?" the children asked. "Will he believe I have been good?"

Santa is happy to see everybody. c. 1980.

Photograph courtesy of Debbie Kramer Broome.

Santa Arrives

Anxious children, dressed in their Sunday best, squirmed and stretched their necks to see if Santa had arrived yet. Then the crowd heard the soft, far-away sound of sleigh bells. The ringing bells grew louder and louder, and the audience's excitement grew as they realized that Santa was coming. The crowd clapped and yelled, "He is here!" Throughout the line, all the way down to the people who stood outside the store, the news spread that Santa had arrived. Those in the Old Dominion Room turned their eyes towards the chimney, and hoped to be the first to spy Santa's black leather boots. As the crowd of hundreds awaited his arrival, first one black leather boot appeared in the chimney and then the other, then his feet dangled for a moment before Santa landed on the fireplace floor. Children gasped as he stood inside the chimney;

Santa standing up and exiting the chimney. c. 1980.

Photograph courtesy of Debbie Kramer Broome.

they saw only the bottom of his coat and his shiny black leather boots. Then Santa bent down, and knelt in the chimney and peeped out. The children saw a wide smile, twinkling eyes, white snowy beard and ruby red cheeks.[45]

Santa looked surprised that so many children had traveled to see him. He was so happy to see all those smiling faces, and from his kneeling position, Santa waved to all. Each member of the audience felt that he waved personally to him or her. He stood up and wiped off the soot from his knees as the audience's cameras went click, click, click. He emerged from the chimney, and what a most glorious sight! Christmas season was officially here. Santa Claus had come down the M&R chimney.

At Miller & Rhoads, the Santa Wonderland did not change year to year; it appeared to be the same Santa in the same clothes. This was a

Santa greeting the children. c. 1980.

Photograph courtesy of Debbie Kramer Broome.

part of the tradition and what made the M&R Santa the Real Santa. No surprises detracted from the authenticity of the M&R Santa Claus. The children and even the parents recognized him. Santa's Christmas suit was made of the finest materials available. The velvet coat was a deep crimson red that made Santa's cheeks look even redder. The fur trim was at least four inches wide and appeared to be so soft and clean. Santa's wide leather belt, from which he hung his white gloves, matched his knee-high, black leather boots. Sitting upon his head was his hat with the white fur ball at the tip.[46]

After he left the chimney, Santa Claus walked to the front of the stage, picked up a microphone and spoke to the waiting crowd. Santa

Santa fixing his beard. c. 1980.

Photograph courtesy of Debbie Kramer Broome.

told the children how glad he was to see them and how good they looked. He called out "Merry Christmas," and asked the children if they were ready for Christmas. All the little children yelled, "Yes!" Santa's face lit up as he explained to the children that they were not the only ones who were excited about Christmas. The reindeer were so excited they could hardly wait.

"Dasher, Dancer, Prancer, Vixen, Comet, Cupid, Donner and Blitzin and yes, Rudolph, away we will all fly, all the way to your home on Christmas Eve," Santa told the audience.

Santa looked at the young visitors and asked if they had thought of what they wanted for Christmas. The children said, "Yes!" or nodded their heads.

Santa calling to the first child in line. c. 1980.
Photograph by Ginny & Sonny McDaniel courtesy of Lisa McDaniel Ramos.

"Well," said Santa, "Then let me get my Snow Queen to come out and then I will find out what you want."

The white door opened, and in walked the Snow Queen and the elf. The elf escorted the Snow Queen to her chair and helped her get comfortable. The elf returned to Santa's side and sat on a stool. Meanwhile, Santa walked to his chair, sat down and put on his white gloves. Santa still needed a few minutes to prepare for the day, so the first child in line moved toward the Snow Queen and talked with her until Santa was ready.

"Little elf, do you have my mirror and comb?" Santa asked.

"Yes," the elf replied and handed them to Santa.

Santa took off his hat and handed it to the elf. The elf hung the red hat on the top corner of Santa's chair. Santa examined himself in the mirror and realized he needed to freshen up his beard and hair. His beard and hair always got messed up from his trip down the chimney. Santa fluffed his beard and combed his hair. When he finished, he looked once into the mirror and asked the elf,

"How do I look, little elf?"

"Fine!" the elf replied.

Santa gazed at himself once more in the mirror, smiled and gave himself a wink. The children laughed and joined in the fun. Santa handed the mirror and comb back to the little elf and motioned to the child standing next to the Snow Queen.

"Hello Megan," Santa said, "Come and visit with me." Parents watched in amazement as Santa called their children by name. There had not been any conversation between the Snow Queen and Santa, nor had Santa asked the children's names. The children accepted for a fact that this Santa knew them. "Of course he knows my name," the youngster thought. "He is the Real Santa, after all."

Santa gently picked up the child, and placed him or her on his lap. As Santa's arm affectionately encircled the child's waist, he told the child how happy he was to see them. This was the moment the children had waited for throughout the whole year. The children had spent hours upon hours contemplating what they wanted for Christmas. For some children, their Christmas list had been in development since the start of the school year and most certainly by Thanksgiving. When they visited with Santa, most children knew exactly what they wanted. Some children wrote their lists down. Mothers and fathers helped the younger children write their lists. The usual Christmas list was very simple and just had a few items on it, such as dolls for girls and cars for boys. But

Santa knew children who turned in lists, which were huge and consisted of many pages. Yet not all children brought lists with them. Some knew exactly what they wanted, and they could remember every detail of their wishes. The very young children were not able to ask for anything in particular. Santa took his time, read each list and listened quietly to the child. Regardless of how the youngster asked for gifts, at the end of the visit, they usually asked for surprises. This complemented Santa's plan since this Santa never promised to deliver anything for which he was specifically asked. He promised to visit them, surprise them and always love them. The whole conversa-tion between Santa and the chil-dren was heard throughout the room because of Santa's hand-held microphone. Proud parents and grandparents heard every word.

Marilyn, Nancy Carolyn and Robin Hood visiting with Santa Claus, 1955.

Courtesy of Frances & Art Hood.

The 10-foot walk from the Snow Queen to Santa was not an easy one for all children. The chil-dren loved him and were excited about the visit while they stood in line, but upon closer examination, Santa scared some children. Santa understood that children were in-dividuals with their own person-alities. Each child approached Santa in a different way. Some children went directly to Santa when he called. Other children hesitated out of fear or shyness. Santa knew which children needed encouragement to cross the stage. Santa worked extra hard to ease their minds and to get them to sit on his lap. Santa called softly to the hesitant children and reassured them that they didn't have to sit on his lap but only needed to tell Santa what they wanted for Christmas. A few children needed to be coaxed forward footstep by footstep. Once the children were close enough to him, Santa engaged them in conversation. As the conversation continued, the children edged closer to Santa, unaware of their movement. Once a child stood next to him, Santa slowly placed his arm around his or her waist and without interrupting the conversation, he lifted the child to his lap. Even if Santa was unable to stop a crying child, parents still requested that a photograph be taken. The Santa picture was quite important and most parents realized that children of certain ages were nervous or scared of Santa. Some parents held their children as the whole family gathered around Santa in order to get the picture. The photograph was another part of the tradition of the M&R Santa Claus.

The M&R Santa displayed the spirit of Christmas through patience and love. He believed all children were good, and that they just pos-

Snow Queen talking with a child. c. 1980.
Photograph by Ginny & Sonny McDaniel
courtesy of Lisa McDaniel Ramos.

Chad Broome going to visit Santa. c. 1980.

Photograph courtesy of Debbie Kramer Broome.

sessed different degrees of goodness. He loved the children who cried or were too scared just as much as the children who walked confidentially up to visit with him.[47]

Unbeknownst to the children, while they talked with Santa, Santa looked out into the crowd and made eye contact with the children's parents. Santa acknowledged the parents with a smile and a nod. This action, combined with the knowledge of all the children's names, ensured the belief in all who saw him that he was indeed the Real Santa Claus.

Parents also experienced the magic of these visits, and they silently thanked this special Santa Claus for his Christmas present to them—a token of love handed to their children. They also thanked him for the memories that he created for them and their children. His spell was so

A collection of front covers souvenirs from the visit to the M&R Santa Claus.
Courtesy of the collection of Frances & Art Hood.

powerful that even after a brief visit with a child, the whole family was affected.

At the end of his conversation with the children, Santa reminded them of the true spirit of Christmas, which was to remember the less fortunate children. When the child hopped down from his lap, Santa said, "Remember that Santa loves you." Santa handed them a small present or piece of candy, and off the children ran to their parents, certain that they had just spoken with the Real Santa.

There was no charge for children to visit Santa. Parents often preserved the special memory, however, by purchasing a photograph of their little ones sitting with Santa; in later years they could also purchase a videotape of the visit.

Dressing up for Santa

Parents savored the special memories stored in those photographs and videos. Children usually looked their best because they were dressed in their finest outfits. Women wore hats and gloves that often matched their purses when they shopped at downtown stores. At Christmas time, M&R customers were dressed beautifully.

Mothers bought special Christmas outfits for the occasion. Most girls had a new dress to wear when they saw Santa and mothers kept those dresses and handed them down to their granddaughters. Many mothers can still describe the dresses that their daughters wore to visit Santa at M&R over the years.

The little girls' Christmas dresses were often colored red, green and gold; they wore stockings, and their feet were tucked into Mary

In 1955, Blanche Burke's grandsons poised for a picture with Santa Claus. From left to right, standing, James Sims, Scott Burke, Penn Burke, Beau Walker and David Burke holding Santa. Sitting down, left to right, Burke Walker and Paul Mennetti.
Photograph courtesy of Milton and Bertha Burke.

Janes or City Sandals (little white leather shoes that had two straps across the foot and perforated holes above the toes). Red and green bows might have decorated their hair. Not all mothers bought expensive store-made dresses. Yet they still made sure their daughters had a proper outfit, however. Some mothers went downtown with a pencil and paper; they took the latest girl's fashion into the dressing room and sketched the dress's design on paper. Material was then bought, and mothers or their friends sewed dresses for the little girls. In later years, "fancier" shops were opened where people shopped for *The* Christmas dress. Even today, little girls on their way to see Santa are frequently dressed in velvet and satin with crinoline underneath.[48]

In addition to the dress, each little girl wore a warm winter coat. Coats from Rothschilds, made from wool and trimmed in blue velvet, were very popular. Some coats had capes attached to the shoulder, and they had small bonnets that matched. Little girls also sometimes wore fur coats with matching hats and muffs. The coats and dresses might have been bought in the children's departments at M&R, Thalhimers, Milby's and the Davis Shop.

In 1999, Penn Burke's daughter got married and invited Santa to her wedding. The seven grandsons poised again in the same order with the same Santa Claus.

Photograph courtesy of Milton and Bertha Burke.

Little boys under six years old frequently wore Eaton Suits, which had a suit jacket with a round keyhole collar worn over a shirt. The shirt's collar also served as a collar for the jacket. Young boys wore short pants and knee-high socks instead of long trousers. After they turned six, boys wore long pants, white shirts, tie, jacket and sometimes a vest.

Everybody was dressed up. People discussed how various children looked. Some children wore costly Victorian outfits that the parents purchased for the occasion, while other children were beautifully turned out in hand-made dresses. In line, parents checked the clothing of the children around them, since people stood in line for hours, and there wasn't much else to do. How the children were dressed was of utmost importance!

You Can Count on Santa

Families were brought together by their shared joy in counting down the days until the visit with Santa. Even as children grew up and moved across the country, this one event reunited families and brought back memories of old. In the Santa line, even college students waited with their parents for the annual Christmas visit that was now a family tradition.[49]

What was so remarkable about this Santa, and what made him so real, was his consistency. Second and third generations of children sat on the M&R Santa's lap, as had their parents. Many families' first visit with the M&R Santa was in the 1940s. Those children now brought their children and grandchildren to see him. Santa loved to see the progression of family photographs that the parents showed him. Those pictures brought tears of happiness and pride to his eyes. Nowhere else in Richmond, or Virginia, or perhaps all of America was Santa so reliable and so beloved. Santa never aged or changed, even during his movement from M&R to Thalhimers to the 6th Street Market Place. Here was one tradition that remained the same, regardless of what happened throughout the world.

Year after year, generations visited this amazing Santa. From 15,000 visitors in 1942 to 25,000-35,000 in 1974, to over 120,000 in 1987, the M&R Legendary Santa Claus was a Richmond institution. Year after year, families planned their annual pilgrimages to Richmond to visit the M&R Santa and sit on his lap. Children traveled from as far away as Florida, Georgia, South Carolina, North Carolina, West Virginia, Maryland, Pennsylvania, New Jersey, Washington, D.C. and Texas to visit Santa Claus in downtown Richmond.[50]

One grandmother and her grandchildren flew from Colorado each year, from 1970 to 1980, just to visit M&R. The grandmother had previously lived in Richmond and had taken her children to see this Santa. She moved west with her family, but she continued the tradition of the M&R Santa with her children's children. She also continued the family tradition of seeing Santa the day after Thanksgiving. It was important to her to make the annual trips east to introduce her grandchildren to the Real Santa who had also delighted their parents.[51]

The Real Meaning of Christmas

As children matured and became skeptical, they tried to figure out if this fellow was the Real Santa. Children tested the realness of Santa's beard by pulling on it. Santa's beard was indeed real, and he frequently ended up with sore cheeks from all the pulling. Remarkably, year after year, Santa knew children's names and remembered small things about them, like the names of their siblings, their schools, and even if they sucked their thumbs. For non-believers, or children who were ambivalent about the realness of Santa, or the parents who didn't believe—all it took was one visit with the M&R Santa, and they were convinced. No human knew all the children's names without asking first or could recognize which children belonged to which parents without some assistance. Watching Santa interact with children warmed even the most stubborn heart.[52]

Santa Claus made sure that all children understood that they needed to think of others. He demonstrated this time and time again through his actions. Santa "taught" the lessons of respect and love through his visits with his special friends. Unfortunately, not all children were physically able to wait in the Santa line for over two hours to visit with him. Some of these children were unable to walk. Nevertheless, Santa made sure they were able to see him.

One Christmas, a sick child wanted to visit the Real Santa Claus and he was very excited about his outing to see Santa. The hearts of his grandparents and parents were heavy with worry. The Santa lines at M&R were extremely long, and the child was physically unable to tolerate the long wait. Santa saw the young child and immediately halted his visits. He explained to all the waiting boys and girls that Santa's special friend had arrived. The family was escorted to the front of the line, and the child was placed on Santa's lap. Nobody protested or complained that this child skipped the long wait in line, for their gift of patience demonstrated the true meaning of Santa Claus and Christmas. The family and members of the audience dried their tears, and then the little child was escorted to the Tea Room, where the family was immediately seated to enjoy lunch with Santa. Nowhere else were children treated with such dignity and respect. This was what Santa has meant to Richmond residents. [53]

Toys for Tots, 1950–1960.　　　　Photograph courtesy of Valentine Richmond History Center.

Santa boarding the train in Ashland, Va. c. 1960

Photograph courtesy of William E. Griffin, Jr., Old Dominion Chapter,
National Railway Historical Society, Richmond, VA.

Chapter Five

Adventures with Santa

The M&R Santa experience was not limited to the Old Dominion Room in the M&R building. Children visited him and saw him on the Santa train and in the M&R Tea Room.

The Richmond, Fredericksburg and Potomac Railroad (RF&P) sponsored a special Santa Train from 1958 to 1971. Eugene "Gene" Luck, RF&P General Manager of Passenger Sales, was instrumental in convincing the M&R Santa to come along for the ride.[54]

The special Santa trains ran on one Saturday each Christmas season. On that day, four Santa trains made the round-trip journey from, Richmond to Ashland, and each train accommodated more than

Eugene "Gene" Luck, RF&P General Manager of Passenger Sales. c. 1960.
Photograph courtesy of William E. Griffin, Jr., Old Dominion Chapter, National Railway Historical Society, Richmond, VA.

1,500 people—1,000 children and 500 parents.[55]

Tickets were sold at the special Santa Claus train ticket booth on the store's second floor in the M&R Youth Center. The initial cost of the ticket was fifty cents per person, and a parent was required to accompany their children. By 1971, the ticket price rose to roughly four dollars per person. Parents made sure they bought their

The Richmond, Fredericksburg and Potomac Engine Car. c. 1960.
Photograph courtesy of William E. Griffin, Jr., Old Dominion Chapter, National Railway Historical Society, Richmond, VA.

Children boarding the Santa train at Broad Street Station. c. 1960.
Photograph courtesy of William E. Griffin, Jr., Old Dominion Chapter, National Railway Historical Society, Richmond, VA.

tickets early, because the tickets sold out very quickly.

The Santa Train originated at the old Broad Street Station. Parents and children would arrive at the station at least half an hour before the train was due to depart. When the conductor yelled, "All aboard!" excited children and their parents walked down the stations steps, gathered on the platform and entered the passenger cars. Children wanted to make sure they could get a window seat. Over the years, the Santa Train grew to include twenty-two passenger cars.

Each passenger car was packed with children and adults. As soon as the train left the station, the entertainment began. Clowns walked through each car and created balloon characters and made the children laugh. Charlie Wakefield, a well-known local musician, led children in singing Christmas carols, as he played his accordion. The M&R Teen Council, which was made up of teenage girls from local high schools, walked from car to car handing out candy canes and entertain-

Train car filled with excited children and their parents. c. 1960.

Photograph courtesy of William E. Griffin, Jr., Old Dominion Chapter, National Railway Historical Society, Richmond, VA.

A clown entertaining the passengers on the Santa Train. c. 1960.
Photograph courtesy of William E. Griffin, Jr.,
Old Dominion Chapter, National Railway Historical Society, Richmond, VA.

Little boy looking for Santa. c. 1960.
Photograph courtesy of William E. Griffin, Jr.,
Old Dominion Chapter, National Railway Historical Society, Richmond, VA.

ing the children. The holiday passengers loved the adventure, because for some, in the age of automobiles, this was their only train trip. The train ride itself excited the children, but as the train approached Ashland, the children became even more anxious to pick up the next passenger.

The weight of the passenger cars seemed to shift uneasily to one side as the train approached Randolph Macon College. Children left no free

"Ho, Ho, Ho!" Santa entering the train car. c. 1960.
Photograph courtesy of William E. Griffin, Jr., Old Dominion Chapter, National Railway Historical Society, Richmond, VA.

space at the windows on the right side of the train, pressing their noses and faces flat against the glass windows. The windows fogged up from the breath of so many youngsters, as they looked for Santa and his Snow Queen. Even the parents gathered at the windows so as not to miss a thing. The train slowed down, and in the distance, the children saw Santa's sleigh with Santa Claus and his Snow Queen directly in front. The train slowed down even more as each of the twenty-two cars rode slowly by Santa. Santa stood tall on the lawn and waved at each car. Finally, when all the passenger cars had gone by except for the last car, the train stopped, and Santa climbed aboard.

As soon as Santa and his Snow Queen were on board, the train started up again and continued to head north to Doswell. All during the journey to Doswell, Santa greeted children. The railroad car door would open and in stepped Santa, who greeted the children with a loud "Merry Christ-

Santa greeting a little child. c. 1960.

Photograph courtesy of William E. Griffin, Jr.,
Old Dominion Chapter, National Railway Historical Society, Richmond, VA.

mas!" Santa said hello to every child and patted heads. The little ones were lucky enough to be picked up and hugged. Children's eyes grew wide as they watched Santa. Parents marveled at his ability to greet each and every one.

In Doswell, the train entered a small railroad loop, and the engine was detached from the front passenger car and reattached to the original last passenger car. After that was completed, the train started up again and headed back to Richmond, with the last car now in the first position. Santa continued his journey through the cars and made sure that all the children saw him. As he left each car, he wished the children well and

Santa waving good-bye as he exits the train car. c. 1960.

Photograph courtesy of William E. Griffin, Jr.
Old Dominion Chapter, National Railway Historical Society, Richmond, VA.

told them to have a Merry Christmas.

When the train entered the Broad Street Station, the children as-sumed that this was the end of the trip. The children exited the train and walked up one of the four staircases to the main hall of the station. At the top of the stairs, the children were surprised to see Santa again. The great central hall contained two rows of benches that faced away from each other and ran down the central aisle. A platform was connected to the backs of the benches. Santa stood on that platform, and called out "Merry Christmas" to all the children as they left the station.

In 1971, the Santa Train trips ended. The National Railroad Passen-ger Corp (Amtrak) took over the RF&P line, but could not provide enough passenger cars. Between 10,000 and 12,500 people had ridden the train each season; totaling more than 100,000 people that the Santa Trains had carried on its holiday adventures.[56]

Santa waves to the children from a platform in the Broad Street Station. c. 1960.
Photograph courtesy of William E. Griffin, Jr.,
Old Dominion Chapter, National Railway Historical Society, Richmond, VA.

Santa and the Snow Queen waving at Broad Street Station. c. 1960.
Photograph courtesy of William E. Griffin, Jr.,
Old Dominion Chapter, National Railway Historical Society, Richmond, VA.

M&R Tea Room Postcard.   Courtesy of Kathryn Fuller-Seeley.

In the Tea Room

The other prime Christmas-time opportunity to visit with Santa was in the M&R Tea Room. Regular Santa visitors learned how to "time" their Santa Land visit in order to leave enough time to eat in the Tea Room with Santa, for just like Santa Land, the Tea Room always had long lines, and M&R never accepted reservations for this event. The Tea Room at Christmas time was part of many family traditions; children visited Santa Land and ate in the Tea Room every Christmas. The M&R Tea Room held very special memories for many Richmonders. Bridal luncheons and wedding showers were often held there, too.

The M&R Tea Room was opened in 1923, along with the completion of the store's expansion. Richmond's downtown district was the cultural and social center of the city. M&R now had 361,900 square feet of selling space, including six floors and a basement. This expansion made M&R the biggest department store in the South between Woodward &

Tea Room Foyer, 5th Floor, c. 1924. Photograph courtesy of Valentine Richmond History Center.

Lothrops' in Washington, D.C. and Rich's in Atlanta. The store occupied the city block of Broad Street and Grace Street (north and south) and 5th and 6th Streets (east and west), except the lower floors at the corner of Broad and 5th Street that housed Woolworth's.[57]

This expansion altered M&R, as the store was transformed into a department store palace. The store had many different departments spread throughout a seven-story building. M&R offered the flavor and ambiance of northern urban department stores. M&R's first floor transported the customer from Richmond to a New York City department store with displays of jewelry, gloves and scarves and the Stag Shop. The second floor, better known as the "Shopping Center of the South," was for the female customer. Women's clothing occupied most of the second floor: dresses, suits, blouses and sweaters. The second floor Virginia Room, like the first floor Stag Shop, salesclerks knew they conducted business with special customers. Walls separated the Virginia Room from the rest of the M&R shop floor. The overall atmosphere of the room suggested a gracious home; it was furnished with thick oriental carpets, velour-covered chairs, wallpapered walls, full-length mirrors and individual service. The Walnut Room was a millinery room where the M&R customer chose a custom-made Sarah Sue hat made specifically for her by Sara Sue Sherrill Waldbauer. She designed the hats exclusively for M&R for over 42 years. When women bought a special dress, they frequently went to Sara Sue for a hat designed to match the new outfit. Mothers and grandmothers also purchased children's clothing for infants through teens here.

The third and fourth floors housed the homemaking departments where customers purchased furniture, art and rugs. Here customers found trained professional salespeople and interior designers ready to help them in selecting living room suites, flooring and bedding. M&R offered classes in sewing and interior decorating. The fourth floor contained a selection of hand-woven rugs from China, Persia, and other exotic places around the world.

The *Richmond Times Dispatch* heralded the fifth floor Tea Room as the most glamorous of all southern tearooms, when the store re-opened after a 1923 remodeling. The Tea Room provided a relaxing atmosphere

The Tea Room was busy during lunch.   Dementi photograph courtesy of Valentine Richmond History Center. 1950-1960.

for the all-day shopper and it mesmerized the customers with three decorated eating rooms: Colonial, English and Italian. After a customer tripped and fell into the fountain in the Italian room, M&R remodeled the three rooms into an all-English theme. The Tea Room quickly became a weekly meeting spot, predominately for women, but also for local businessmen. A trio of musicians played live music daily from 12:15 to 2:45 p.m. until 1939, when Eddie Weaver was engaged to play live piano and organ music at lunchtime and for special occasions.[58]

Customers sat on upholstered, hand-carved wooden chairs at linen-covered tables with china place settings, which set the elegant ambiance of the room. Chandeliers provided light as plants and decorations hid the structural columns. Hand-painted murals, decorated with scenes of

The Tea Room Christmas children's menu.

Courtesy of Jody Weaver Wampler.

old-fashioned ladies and gentlemen of the 1880's, covered the walls. Patrons of the Tea Room wore their Sara Sue hats and proper attire, for both customers and employees completed the elegant feeling of the Tea Room. As the women dined on club sandwiches, chicken salad plates, soups, fresh vegetables and fruits, M&R models wearing the latest New York fashions strolled along the runway down the middle of the room. After walking the runway, the models roamed the Tea Room floor and talked to the customers about their outfits.[59]

It was in this elegant atmosphere that children dined with Santa during the holiday season. At lunch and dinnertime from the day after Thanksgiving through Christmas Eve, Santa ate in the Tea Room with

Waiting in line to get a seat in the Tea Room. Notice the signs above the children's head; the signs indicated which line to wait in. 1950-1960.

Dementi photograph courtesy of Valentine Richmond History Center.

children and their parents. The Tea Room's regular patrons did not usually include youngsters, especially children under the age of eight or nine, who might be left behind at home or at a friend's house while their mothers shopped. The very fact that the children were invited to eat in the Tea Room was excitement enough; most children understood that it was a privilege, and they behaved themselves.

During the Christmas holiday season, children made up at least half

Santa greets the children. c. 1980.
Photograph courtesy of Frances & Art Hood.

of the Tea Room's patrons. Not one thing about the Tea Room was changed for the young diners; the very elegance of the Tea Room remained unchanged. The tables were still set with china on linen table clothes. The children were expected to know and display proper table etiquette.

Immediately after the children saw Santa Claus, the family rushed off to the Tea Room. No reservations were accepted for this busy event, so in order to be seated, families got in line quite early.

Mirroring the long queues upstairs to see Santa, the Tea Room crowd lined up one to two hours before the actual seating time at lunch or

Santa hands out Rudolph cake. c. 1960.   Photograph courtesy of Dementi Studio.

dinner. Outside of the Tea Room, lines were separated according to the number of people in the lunch or dinner party: Tables for 2, Tables for 3, Tables for 4 and Tables for More, which enabled the Tea Room hostess to seat people more efficiently. Once the Tea Room opened, hundreds of excited children hoped to get a seat at a table close to the runway. Within minutes the Tea Room was filled to capacity, and the ropes were laid across the doorways causing long lines, once more, to snake throughout the fifth floor.

Those who were lucky enough to enter the Tea Room saw a room decorated for the holidays with the sounds of Christmas music coming from the beautiful organ music being played by Eddie Weaver. He led

Santa telling the children not to drink their milk like he does. c. 1980.
Photograph courtesy of Debbie Kramer Broome.

the children in singing familiar Christmas carols while they waited for Santa and the Snow Queen; favorites were "Rudolph the Red Nose Reindeer," "Jingle Bells," and "Here Comes Santa Claus."

The Tea Room had a special children's Christmas menu, offering cheeseburgers, sandwiches and other entrées that suited children's tastes. Children's eyes followed the long runaway up to the end of the stage, where a table was set for Santa and his Snow Queen. Santa's table was directly centered in front of white panels, painted and decorated to resemble a house. A large round wreath hung in the center panel. The elf

Santa drinking his milk. c. 1980.   Photograph courtesy of Debbie Kramer Broome.

sat at a separate table to the Snow Queen's right. The elf's roundtable had a red and green tablecloth.

Families ordered their meals as they waited for Santa's arrival. Around 11:30 a.m., Eddie Weaver started to play "Jingle Bells," and in walked Santa. He entered the room on the stage. Santa called to the back of the room and his Snow Queen and elf entered, walking through the crowd and waving to the children, calling them by name. The elf followed with a bouncy step and smiled all the way to the runway. The Snow Queen and elf joined Santa at the end of the runway. Santa took the Snow Queen's

Santa eating lunch with his Snow Queen. c. 1980.
Photograph by Ginny & Sonny McDaniel courtesy of the collection of Lisa McDaniel Ramos.

hand and escorted her to the table. Once there, Santa pulled out her chair and helped her into her seat. He then walked to the microphone set up on stage.

Santa always began his visit with a special greeting. He reminded the children that he was very excited to see them and exclaimed how pretty and handsome they all looked.

Santa repeated the story of the excited reindeer, who couldn't wait to fly to the children's homes on Christmas Eve. This version of his story was different, because he added a story about Rudolph. It seemed that

Rudolph loved to help out in any way possible. One of Rudolph's favorite activities was helping Santa make a cake. Rudolph used his hooves to mix the cake's batter. Children were on the edge of their seats, as Santa went on. He told them that he had some of that cake that Rudolph had helped make right there in the Tea Room. Slices of the famous Rudolph cake were set on two five-foot long tables, which had been placed at the end of the runway. Each table held many slices of cake. Santa asked the children if they wanted some of that cake, and of course the room erupted in affirmative cries!

Eddie Weaver played "Rudolph the Red Nose Reindeer" as Santa walked down the runway toward the cake. Santa asked the children to meet him at the front table, so they could receive a piece of cake. From all corners of the Tea Room, children hurried toward the cake table. They didn't rush in and grab their piece of cake, but waited till Santa came down the runway steps and stood behind the table. Santa handed out the Rudolph cake, and children stood five deep around the table waiting to get their piece. Before Santa handed it out, he reminded the children to return to their seats after they received a piece of cake, and in that way, everyone was assured of receiving a piece of the Rudolph Cake.[60]

While Santa was busy handing out cake with both hands the kitchen staff brought out more cake slices. Once all the children were back in their seats, Santa called out to make sure that everyone had a piece. When he was sure, he went back up the runway stairs and walked back to his table at the end of the stage. Santa looked out over the crowded room and smiled at all the children enjoying their special desserts. He removed his hat and placed it on the table. Then he took off his white gloves and tucked them into his belt. Immediately he saw the glass of milk on the table. Santa looked surprised and smiled at the audience. He picked up the glass of milk and told the children not to drink their milk as he did, or they would have a bellyache. Eddie Weaver played on the organ as Santa drank down all his milk without stopping for air. Santa placed the glass down on the table, put his hands on his stomach and gave a deep laugh that shook his famous belly. Then he sat down and enjoyed his lunch.

While Santa dined, he waved and nodded to the children. Santa took special care to acknowledge the children in the back of the room. These children might not have believed that Santa could see them, but Santa made eye contact, nodded or waved to each child.

Eddie Weaver playing the piano for his young fans. 1983.
Photograph couresty of Paul Bates.

When he was finished eating, Santa stood up, stretched and put his hat back on. It was time to return to the seventh floor and visit with more children. Yet, while Santa ate his meal, many children had finished theirs, and new children had been seated. So when it was time for Santa to leave, he repeated his story about Rudolph and the cake. Once more, Santa went down to the Rudolph Cake at the end of the runway and asked if there was anyone who missed getting a piece the first time around, and he handed out slices to those children. Santa then walked to the front entrance of the Tea Room and

Eddie Weaver dressed as a train conductor "driving" his train at the Loews Theater.   Photograph courtesy of Jody Weaver Wampler.

exited. As he left to return to his throne, he walked by the waiting line of children and told them about the Rudolph cake awaiting them.

Eddie Weaver adds
to the Tradition

A big part of lunch with Santa and Christmas at M&R was Eddie Weaver, the famous local organist, who also played at Loew's Theater directly across 6th Street from the store. The visit to the Tea Room and Eddie at Christmas became a family tradition, and parents traveled from out-of-state to bring their children.[61]

Edward "Eddie" Weaver was born in Catasauqua, Pennsylvania. He

Jody and Eddie Weaver playing for the Tea Room lunch crowd.

Dementi photograph. Photograph courtesy of Jody Weaver Wampler.

was the son of Mr. and Mrs. Edward P. Weaver, who were musically inclined; Weaver learned to play the piano from his mother, who was a music teacher. Weaver had planned to study church and concert organ at the Eastman School of Music in Rochester, New York, but changed his mind when he was hired to play in movie theaters. In 1928, Weaver settled in New Haven, Connecticut, and accompanied silent movies and stage shows on the organ.[62]

In 1936, Loew's Theater transferred him to Richmond, and in 1939, Weaver was hired by Webster Rhoads, Jr. to perform at the Tea Room. No description of M&R was complete without mention of Weaver's performances on the piano and organ. Weaver became a Richmond legend.

In his programs at Loew's Theater it wasn't only Weaver's music that entertained the people. Weaver, himself, was also quite an entertainer. He made the audience part of the show through his direct interaction with them in sing-a-longs. He studied his audiences and adjusted his music to fit the crowd; he played in the key that best suited Richmond voices, the one between middle and high C. If he believed the audience was too serious, he cued the control room to run tongue-twisting lyrics on the screen. He played birthday songs and sent out special greetings to members of the audience. He memorized over 3,600 songs to play, which included everything from popular numbers to parodies of old tunes; he enjoyed working up parodies that commented on local subjects. Weaver's showmanship included a

Eddie Weaver points to a song Jody wrote and was published in **The Mighty Theatre Organ**.

Photograph courtesy of Jody Weaver Wampler.

few tricks. His last chord was usually identical or in tune with the first notes of the sound track of the feature film that followed his program. He could even play a different tune with each hand and a third with his feet on the organ pedals!

Weaver also had his own morning radio program on WRNL, broadcast from 11:00-11:30 a.m. Monday through Friday. Occasionally, he had a youth talent segment on the show that showcased local youngsters. The most promising young musicians were invited to play with him at Loew's.

Weaver did not include sing-a-longs in his Tea Room performances during lunch, but he knew how to work the Tea Room crowd; he accepted requests throughout lunch. For a time in the 1960s, the theme from "Dr. Zivago" was his most requested song.

Tea Room models walked down the runway accompanied by Weaver's music. Weaver had a great relationship with the models, and he had special tunes that signaled to the models that they needed to move quicker or that the boss had arrived, and they needed to behave.

Weaver was part of the Tea Room family. He knew the customers who ate in the Tea Room every day. One group of men, who sat at the same table near Weaver every day, even gave their group a name, "The Table by the Organ," and everyone knew that was their special lunch table.

Weaver enjoyed the Christmas holidays. He usually wore a dark colored jacket and a tie, but at Christmas time, he wore a red or green jacket with a holiday tie.

Weaver's first recording was made in 1958, an album of holiday tunes titled "Eddie Weaver Plays Christmas Music." It was Richmond's first professionally produced LP. One side of his album was aimed at children. He played songs in a tempo that made them easy to sing, including "Jingle Bells," "Frosty the Snowman," "Sleigh Ride," "Parade of Wooden Soldiers," "Rudolph the Red Nosed Reindeer," "Santa Claus is Coming to Town" and "Mr. and Mrs. Santa Claus" (composed by Mildred Hyde of Richmond). On the flip side, Weaver spun yule time music with more of an adult appeal. Eddie and his daughter, Jody, played instrumental versions of such classic carols as "Joy to the World," "Hark the Herald Angels Sing," "O! Little Town of Bethlehem" and "Adeste Fidelis."

The M&R Fawn Shop.   Photograph courtesy of Valentine Richmond History Center.

In 1985 Eddie Weaver and Santa produced a second recording of Christmas music. The music was by Eddie Weaver and his daughter sang. The recording included "I'm Dreaming of a White Christmas," "Rudolf the Red Nose Reindeer," "Silver Bells" and twelve other songs.[57]

Eddie Weaver was as much a part of the M&R Tea Room through the year as Santa Claus was during the holidays. No meal was complete, unless Weaver played live music. Children loved Eddie Weaver, and some even referred to him as Uncle Eddie. Sometimes Eddie Weaver allowed the children to sit beside him on the organ or piano bench, unless they interfered with his music.

Fawn Shop, a more modern version. c. 1980.

Photograph by Ginny & Sonny McDaniel courtesy of the collection of Lisa McDaniel Ramos.

The Fawn Shop

Children were central to the celebration of Christmas at M&R. After the visit with Santa and eating in the Tea Room, children shopped in a "store" created just for them. Just like the Stag Shop, which was only for their daddies, the Fawn Shop was only for children. The Fawn Shop was located on the children's floor. Parents waited outside the shop in chairs, while children shopped for presents for the whole family. Children stood in line, since the Fawn Shop limited the number of children entering at any one time. Inside the Fawn Shop M&R employees helped the children with their purchases and went out of the store to ask the children's parents for assistance, if a little more money was needed to pay the bill. Some parents simplified the buying process by giving the child their M&R charge cards. The parents would note on a piece of paper the child's spending limit, and the employee would help keep the children within their budgets.[63]

The store employees must have felt like giants inside the Fawn Shop, for everything within it was diminutive the store's entrance was at children's height, and all the display counters were child size. M&R employees had to bend at the knees to help the little shoppers.

A wide range of merchandise was available for purchase. Socks, ties, soaps, pens and pencils, hankies, scarves, knick-knacks, boxes to hold jewelry and key rings all manner of little things that were not too expensive but which appealed to a child. Perfume was a favorite gift for mothers. Children usually chose them for the pretty boxes more than for the actual

Bruce the Spruce. c. 1980.
Photograph courtesy of Debbie Kramer Broome.

perfume scent. The presents were priced just for children's budgets; most gifts cost less than one dollar. Some children bought what they needed and "budgeted" to have enough money left over to purchase something sweet for themselves. Children who didn't have enough money for that something extra often bought mom or dad a combined gift of candy, knowing that parents usually shared.

The employees wrapped up the presents, and the children left the Fawn Shop with their own little bags. It was a very important event for children to do their own shopping.

Bruce the Spruce

On the third floor, Bruce the Spruce stood in the children's department. Bruce held court in the center of a white picket fence with a forest behind him. Bruce's height reached 8-10 feet, and his branches were decorated with a wide assortment of Christmas decorations. The Bruce's magic happened only at Christmas time, when he left the forest and traveled with Santa to M&R. Once at the store, Bruce magically came alive. Bruce talked, sang and interacted with people, just as well as any person could; even his lips moved as he spoke. Bruce loved children. The Christmas season was his favorite season because he saw all his friends from the previous years. He greeted his friends by name, just like Santa. Children liked to watch Bruce's lips move as he spoke to them. The children talked right back to him as if he were real. Bruce also liked to have fun and sometimes caught unsuspecting people by surprise. Not everyone believed that a tree could come to life, and so they walked right by him. Imagine their shock when Bruce spoke! Bruce also liked to sing. He often asked the children what they wanted to hear, and then he joined them in singing carols. The most requested song, of course, was "Jingle Bells."[64]

After visiting with Santa, lunch in the Tea Room, seeing Bruce the Spruce and shopping in the Fawn Shop, the family might have spent the whole day at M&R. Christmas, in so many ways, was unlike any other time of the year.

Santa on his way to visit the residents at the Virginia Home. Santa's friend Charlotte rides along as Milton Burke transports Santa around town.
Photograph courtesy of Milton Burke.

Chapter Six

Santa's Special Gift from the Heart

M&R's Santa was an extremely busy fellow. He seldom ventured outside the doors of the store. Other than his ride on the Santa Train, Santa left the store for only two occasions— he lit the Governor's Mansion Christmas Tree in Capital Square, and he visited sick children.

Santa switched on the Christmas tree at the Governor's Mansion shortly after his arrival, on the Saturday following Thanksgiving. This marked the beginning of the Christmas season for Richmonders.[65]

The Legendary Santa Claus rarely traveled during the Christmas holidays, yet he knew what went on in children's lives throughout the year. Santa contacted people throughout the year if he felt certain families needed special help.

Santa felt it was important to share the spirit of Christmas with boys and girls who were unable to travel to M&R to see him in person. All children deserved to celebrate the joys of Christmas, and a personal visit from Santa ensured that they were not forgotten children, but special in their own ways. Children in hospitals, orphanages and shut-ins at home

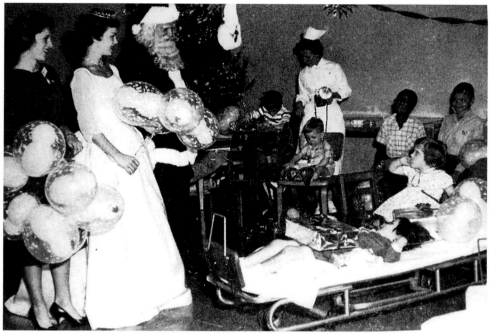

Santa visiting children in the hospital. c. 1960. **M&R Mirror**.
Photograph courtesy of Valentine Richmond History Center.

were amazed and delighted when Santa appeared at their door. Santa handed out presents, and he also gave gifts of hope and love. Today, Santa still visits the Virginia Home bringing gifts to all the residents.[66]

Unfortunately, even Santa's visits could not heal all children. On one occasion a little boy was very ill and did not have much longer to live. His last wish was to meet Santa. He was physically unable to go to the M&R store, so Santa went to the boy's house to visit him several days prior to his usual Christmas Eve drop-by. Santa made the boy's last Christmas wish come true. Christmas was giving to others in ways that words could not express.[67]

Santa visited sick and underprivileged children, and in this way he was able to spend more time with them than he normally could at the store. Santa's smile or wink motivated the children to try harder and to get better. He told them tales about the North Pole and Rudolph.[68]

One treasured story of Santa's care and kindness involved a family who created the Christmas tradition of visiting the Legendary Santa year after year. Unfortunately, the family was transferred to another state, but they had relatives in Richmond and were able return each Christmas to visit the M&R Santa Claus. One summer, after their yearly holiday visit to Richmond, the father of the family passed away. The family was quite upset, but a remarkable thing happened. On the day of the funeral the phone rang, and on the other end of the line was the Legendary Santa. He knew about the father's death and called to let the family know that he was thinking of them and sent his love to them in this sad time.[69]

Santa answers some important questions

A few years ago, a reporter for the weekly Caroline County, newspaper, *Caroline-Progress*, interviewed the M&R Santa. Their conversation centered on the subject of children. A big concern in the minds of many boys and girls was the reindeer. Children worried that the reindeer got tired and hungry from pulling the sleigh on such a long trip. Santa couldn't agree more; he told the children to leave out a carrot with their Santa snack. Rudolph needed extra carrots since he had helped to prepare the Rudolph Cake. Another question children had was how Santa could reach everybody's house, all around the world, in one night. Santa tried to explain that not all countries celebrated Christmas on the same night, and with the time zone changes, he actually had more time than he needed. But, if Santa came down the chimney and saw that the children were still wide awake, he left and came back later, so it was very important that the children be asleep on Christmas Eve. Although children knew that the M&R Santa was the real one, they occasionally asked Santa about all those other Santas whom they saw in other places all over town. Santa explained that those were "Santa's helpers" and that they were normal humans dressed up for the occasion. Without them, he explained, Santa couldn't live in Richmond between Thanksgiving and Christmas Eve. The helpers made sure that those children in other parts of the city, state and country could communicate with Santa. While Santa's helpers were only humans in costume, the North Pole elves were very real. The elves were extremely busy during the Christmas season, but they enjoyed their work, since they knew that their efforts made many people happy.[70]

The reporter asked, "What does Christmas mean to the Legendary Santa Claus?" "Happiness is Christmas," he replied. The reason he delivered toys to children was to make children happy. Happy children made happy parents.

Santa has helped hundreds of thousands of Richmond children and parents understand Christmas and the magic of the season. The M&R Santa has made Christmas special. As one person wrote in his letter to Santa, "Last night was really one of the most incredible, exciting experiences of my entire life… Thank you for making my Christmas what I always wanted it to be as a child."

Christmas Gift Bar, 1950-1960.

Photograph courtesy of Valentine Richmond History Center.

Kathy L. Shuart, age eighteen months, and Santa.
Photograph courtesy of Christine and Gregory Shuart.

Chapter Seven

Saving Santa

The department store industry saw wrenching changes in the 1980's. Proud local chains across the nation struggled in vain to remain profitable. Some merged with giant corporations, while others succumbed. M&R management tried hard to remain afloat through buybacks, reorganization and expansion, growing to fourteen stores in Virginia and one in North Carolina. In the summer of 1989, M&R management announced the possibility of the Richmond store closing, and in 1990, the store permanently closed. A Richmond tradition and era ended.[71]

Richmonders panicked, as they believed that Santa, who had lived here for 45 years, would move on to another city. If Santa could not visit with children at M&R, where could he go? Santa received letters as early as July and August 1989 from parents and children who wanted to know where he was going to relocate for the upcoming season. Some people enclosed stamped and self-addressed envelopes, so that Santa would write them and inform them of his next home. Richmond residents knew that

Elf dancing with children at the Santa lunch at 6th Street Market Place. c. 1990.

Photograph courtesy of Debbie Kramer Broome.

regardless of where he was, he was the only Real Santa. He had taught Richmond the beauty and magic of Christmas. Santa was too important to lose.[72]

As M&R top management scrambled around and looked for investors to save the store, some concerned citizens scrambled around and sought a new home for Santa. Record numbers of people came to see Santa on November 24, 1989, the opening day of the M&R Santa season. By 8:00 a.m. when the store's doors opened, the line for Santa stretched around the entire city block. The line of waiting children and parents took over the sixth and seventh floors, and wound itself through the scarce merchandise. Children and adults waited over three hours to visit with Santa; the line was made of generations of families who had visited with this Santa. Parents, who had grown up with this Santa, felt that it was their obligation to introduce their little ones to the "Real

Santa." Naturally, their children were dressed in suits, dresses and matching outfits for siblings.

The store estimated that between 60,000 to 70,000 people visited with Santa that last year and 50,000 to 60,000 ate Rudolph cake in the Tea Room. By contrast, across the street, at Thalhimers, the line averaged 19 children and adults.[73]

Finally, Christmas Eve arrived, which meant that Santa's stay in Richmond had come to an end. The Christmas Eve crowd was huge and consisted of many of the same families who had come downtown on Christmas Eve for many years. On this night, Santa's visiting hours was shortened, but he still saw all children who stood in line. As the day wound down, the crowd inside the room had grown. Nobody left after his or her visit with Santa; instead they waited in the seating area. Christmas Eve was the only time Santa Claus went back up the chimney. When it looked like the last person had come through the line, Santa stood up and called out to make sure that he had seen everybody. He didn't want to miss a single child. Santa looked around the room at all the people and told them he still had lots of work to do tonight, and it was time he left.

"All of you be good as you can and go to sleep early tonight. I will be coming by." And then the Legendary Santa placed his finger on his nose and recited from the old poem:

"Laying a finger aside his nose, and giving a nod, up the chimney he rose."

Santa walked to the chimney, put on his hat, turned to the Christmas Eve crowd and waved.

"Bye Bye" he said as he went up the chimney and was gone.

The audience clapped heartily and began to button their coats for the journey home and the wait for Christmas morning to come.

The Snow Queen walked to Santa's chair, picked up the microphone and said, "And I heard him exclaim as he flew out of sight…"

Off in the distance, snowbells jingled, and Santa called out one last time,

"Merry Christmas to all and to all a good night."

At 5:30 p.m. on Christmas Eve, 1989, the M&R Santa placed his finger on the side of his nose and went up the chimney for the last time. After 105 years, the M&R era had come to an end.

Yet Richmond's citizens were unwilling to let their M&R tradition end. Even though they had lost a favorite store, customers fought to keep the M&R Santa in Richmond. M&R and Santa were a family tradition that had been passed down from generation to generation. Memories of "the good old days" and Santa were deeply embedded in Richmond's society and memory.

M&R employees saved the famous M&R Clock from the auction block. The clock symbolized the past, when young and old met their friends under the first floor clock and then ventured into a world of shopping. The former M&R employees pooled their resources to purchase the M&R clock, which they donated to the Valentine Museum. At this museum, which focuses on Richmond's heritage, the clock stands out as a proud reminder of something great in Richmond's past.[74]

Fortunately, as it turns out, Richmond never had to celebrate Christmas without the M&R Legendary Santa Claus, for the citizens of Rich-

Santa warming his tired toes by the hot fire the day after Christmas.   Photograph courtesy of Frances & Art Hood.

mond convinced Santa to stay. The following year, Thalhimers Department Store offered Santa Claus their downtown store for the four holiday weeks. Santa agreed, and his original M&R living room set was moved into Thalhimers. Santa celebrated Christmas in the same gold chair, with the Snow Queen, the elf and "Bruce the Spruce." Thalhimer's Snow Bear was a great addition to this traditional setting. Unfortunately, in 1992, Thalhimer's also closed. Once more, however, Richmonders were lucky, and the M&R Santa and his set lived on during the holiday season through the efforts of *Downtown Presents* at the 6th Street Market Place.[75]

Downtown Presents' mission was to keep Santa downtown. Santa was still in the Thalhimers building at the 6th Street Market Place for the 2000 Christmas season. The visit was still free, and parents still bought photographs or a videotape of the visit. It was very important to *Downtown Presents* to keep the Christmas set and characters exactly the same, as people, and Santa, wanted it to continue to look like his living room.

M&R's Santa Claus is still very much a family tradition. Families continue to come downtown on the same day each year, the morning after Thanksgiving. That morning, the line still forms as early as 7 a.m. just as it did years before. Children dress up in their Sunday best, eat lunch with Santa, and have a piece of the Rudolph Cake together. Remarkably, parents travel long distances and bring their children to visit with him. In the Christmas 2000 season, 25 percent of Santa's 20,000 visitors traveled from North Carolina and another 25 percent came from the Tidewater region of Virginia.

Santa remains a part of their families' Christmas celebration, just as much as the Christmas tree and presents. Unfortunately, not many new Richmonders or people who have moved to the outlying areas know that Richmond is lucky enough to have the Real Santa Claus in town. New area residents may not know the history of the store or even the history of the Real Santa Claus, but one visit with him will guarantee that they will believe that this is truly the only Real Santa Claus.

Santa feeding his reindeer. December 26, every year.   Photograph courtesy of the collection of Frances & Art Hood.

Family Photographs with the Legendary Santa Claus

Personalize your book mounting your own photographs with Santa.

Family Photographs with the Legendary Santa Claus

Personalize your book mounting your own photographs with Santa.

Family Photographs with the Legendary Santa Claus

Personalize your book mounting your own photographs with Santa.

Family Photographs with the Legendary Santa Claus

Personalize your book mounting your own photographs with Santa.

Family Photographs with the Legendary Santa Claus

Personalize your book mounting your own photographs with Santa.

Endnotes

Chapter One

1 *M&R Bibliography*, (1960), M&R Records, Valentine Richmond History Center (VRHC); *Golden Jubilee: 50 Years of Progressive Merchandising* (Richmond, Virginia, M&R, 1935), M&R Records, (VRHC); *50 Golden Years* presented to W.S. Rhoads by Richmond Times Dispatch (1935), M&R Records, (VRHC); and William S. Lacy, Jr., "M&R: A Virginia Institution," *The Commonwealth: The Magazine of Virginia* (June 1958) pp. 26-31 and 49-50.

2 Webster S. Rhoads was born May 26, 1858 to Isaac and Hannah Rhoads in Birdsboro, Pennsylvania. Rhoads' educational background consisted of local regional schools and Pleasant Preparatory School. Once he finished school, he began his retail career in a small country store. He went on to become the men's furnishings department manager at Dives, Pomeroy and Stewart in Reading, Pennsylvania. *The National Cyclopedia: American Biography*, Volume XXXI, (New York, James T. White & Co., 1944), p. 162-163 and *Miller-Rhoads News*, 1:5 (September 17, 1941), Box 3, M&R Records, (VRHC). Linton O. Miller was born in Reading, Pennsylvania on December 4, 1860, the son of David and Marie Miller. He began working at Dives, Pomeroy & Stewart as a clerk at the age of fourteen. *National Cyclopedia: American Biography*, Volume XLVII, (New York, James T. White & Co., 1944), p. 632.

3 Lawrence W. Levine's *Highbrow Lowbrow: The Emergence of Cultural Hierarchy in America* (Cambridge, MA, Harvard University Press, 1988); Richard S. Tedlow, *New and Improved: The Story of Mass Marketing in America* (New York, Basic Books, 1990), pp. 3-21; William Leach, *Land of Desire: Merchants, Power, and the Rise of a New American Culture* (New York, Vintage Books, 1994), pp. 20-26; Keith L. Bryant, Jr. and Henry C. Dethloff, *A History of American Business* (Englewood Cliffs, New Jersey, Prentice-Hall, Inc, 1990), pp. 322-324; and E. Anthony Rotundo's, *American Manhood: Transformations in Masculinity from the Revolution to the Modern Era* (New York, Basic Books, 1993) pp.209-211.

4 "Modern store began as Lone room in 1885," *Richmond Times Dispatch* (RTD), (February 17, 1935), and Authors interview with Milton Burke (June 1997, long time M&R employee) and John West, (June 1997).

5 Marie Tyler-McGraw, *At The Falls, Richmond, Virginia, & Its People* (Chapel Hill & London, The University of North Carolina Press, 1994), pp. 184-217; Harry Ward, *Richmond, An Illustrated History* (Northridge, CA, Windsor Publications, 1985) pp. 147-234; and *Chataignes Directory of Richmond, Virginia 1885* (J.H. Chataignes, compiler and publisher, printed at Steam Printing House, Richmond, VA, 1886).

6 *Golden Jubilee*; "W. S. Rhoads Jr. Named Head of Local Department Store," RTD (February 6, 1940), p. 17; John Lee, "M&R Diamond Jubilee Opens," *Richmond News Leader* (RNL), (February 1, 1960), p. 15; "Window Unveiling to Set Stage for Golden Jubilee," RNL (February 16, 1935), p 16; *Chataignes Directory of Richmond, Virginia 1885*; M&R Bankruptcy Files, (File 17); and Ward, pp. 386-387.

7 Virginia Institute Commission, *Richmond, Virginia, 1917: A Glance at Her History* (1917), p. 66.

8 Opening Day Advertisement, *The State* (Richmond, Virginia, October 17, 1885), Box 11, M&R Records, (VRHC).

9 Postcard, Box 13, M&R Records, (VRHC); and Letter from J. Ambler Johnston to Mr. Edwin Hyde (April 18, 1963), which included the cutout advertisement from the Confederate Reunion of 1896, Box 13, M&R Records, (VRHC).

10 William S. Lacy Jr., "M&R: A Virginia Institution," *The Commonwealth: The Magazine of Virginia* (June 1958), pp. 26-50; and "W.S. Rhoads Jr. Named Head of Local Department Store," RTD (February 6, 1940), p 17.

11 W.S. Rhoads letter to William Grant Swartz, Esq. (July 13, 1888) and W.S. Rhoads letter to William Grant Swartz, Esq. (July 19, 1888), Box 10, M&R Records, (VRHC); William Grant Swartz Memorial Program, (December 31, 1935), Box 13, M&R Records, (VRHC). I do not have a copy of the letter sent from Swartz to Rhoads, although the second letter from Rhoads was a response to questions from Swartz.

12 *Chataignes Directory of Richmond, Virginia* (Richmond, VA, 1885-1887); *J.C. Hill's Directory of Richmond & Manchester, Virginia* (J.L. Printing Co, Richmond, VA, 1888 to 1900); "Window Unveiling to Set Stage for Golden Jubilee," RNL (February 16, 1935), p. 5; and Lacy Jr., pp. 26-50.

13 Douglas S. Freeman's editorial in RNL (April 27, 1917), M&R Records, (VRHC).

14 M&R advertisement, RTD (December 15, 1923), p. 20; M&R advertisement, "The Story of a Shopping Center", RTD (December 22, 1923) back page; M&R advertisement, "North! —South! —East! —West! —," RNL (December 15, 1923) p. 3; "M&R Open New Grace Street Annex," RNL (November 30, 1923), p. 27; and "M&R: The Shopping Center" advertisement, RNL (December 5, 1923), p. 3.

15 Postcard to Mr. Rhoads from Arthur W. Bates, M&R Buyer (1923) Box 10, M&R Records, (VRHC); M&R advertisement, "Christmas Gifts From All Over the World," RNL (December 5, 1923); and M&R advertisement, RNL (November 30, 1923), p. 3.

16 Golden Jubilee Scrapbook; "M&R Unveiling to set stage for Golden Jubilee: Gala occasion planned for 8 tonight, to Show New Styles," RNL (February 27, 1935) p. 4; Employee Association Meetings (1935), Box 10, M&R Records, (VRHC); Employee Association Meetings (minutes August 28, 1937), Box 3, M&R Records, (VRHC). *The Drivers Manual Store Rules, Safety Rules, and Bonus System of 1930* booklet explained the bonus system for drivers.

17 *M&R Bibliography*, pp. 35-36; "W.S. Rhoads will Serve in Air Corps," RTD

(May 16, 1942), p. 17; and "Memorial to A.B. Laughon, Vice President and General Manager," *The Mirror* 4:1 (July 7, 1944), Box 3, M&R Records, (VRHC).

18 *M&R Annual Reports to Stockholders*, years 1948 to 1959, Box 1, M&R Records, (VRHC). Following endnotes from the Annual reports are written: *Annual* (year) unless otherwise noted.

19 *Annual* (1955), *Annual* (1956) and *Annual* (1957).

20 *Annual* (1955), *Annual* (1956) and *Annual* (1958).

21 *Annual* (1954).

22 *Annual* (1960 to 1966); Pembroke Mall Opening, Box 13, M&R Records, (VRHC); *Confidential Store Manager Releases*, LI (March 9, 1965), XLV (May 31, 1962), and LII (July 3, 1965) Box 12, M&R Records, (VRHC); and M&R Roanoke Downtown, Box 13, M&R Records, (VRHC).

23 Pamphlet "M&R and Richmond, is only part of the picture," (c.1960); population figure courtesy of Richmond Chamber of Commerce, all other figures courtesy of Richmond newspapers, M&R 1950 folder, (VRHC); *The Governor's Awards for the Arts* (program, 1979), Box 12, M&R Records, (VRHC); and *The Mirror*, 3:4 (November 1953), Box 3, M&R Records, (VRHC). Nelson Hyde, "One-Horse Wagon Stars in M&R Jubilee," RNL (February 2, 1960), p. 15. Robert Price worked for M&R from 1911 to 1957.

24 M&R bag (with quote), Box 13, M&R Records, (VRHC); Webster S. Rhoads Jr. Speech, *75 years of Growth*" (New York, Newcomen Society in North America, 1960), Box 9, M&R Records, (VRHC); and W. M. Harper to Mr. William Ellyson, (January 24, 1956), Box 13, M&R Records. For the store's policy, see *1916 M&R Rules Book*, p. 1, Box 10, M&R Records, (VRHC).

25 M&R began a monthly house magazine in July 1910 called *The M&R Monthly Record*. As president, Rhoads wrote the opening editorials of each issue, where he emphasized customer service. *The M&R Montly Record* will change its name many times, the title *The M&R Mirror*, was the last and the one most M&R employees were familiar with. In November 1910, Rhoads' article "Live Up to the Best That's in You" stressed his thoughts on customer service, Box 3, M&R Records (VRHC); *M&R Rules and Regulations for the Guidance of Employees years 1888, 1914, 1916, 1917*, Box 10, M&R Records, (VRHC); C.M. Harrison, "Educating the Retailer by Instructing His Sales Force," *Printer's Ink Monthly* (May 1922), p. 21; For *the Information and Counsel of the New Employees of M&R* (published by M&R, 1927); and *Store System and General Store Rules* (published by M&R, 1927), Box 10, M&R Records, (VRHC).

26 Letter to all Sales Managers from Emion Smith, Training Director (October 17, 1958), Box 13, M&R Records, (VRHC).

27 "We Have the First Victory Garden Run by a Store," *The Mirror*, 2: 3 (July 13, 1942), and "M&R Sells War Bonds," *The Mirror*, 3: 4 (September 13, 1941), Box 13, M&R Records, (VRHC); "Let's Back the Attack," *The Mirror*, 3: 8 (January 26,1944), "4th War Loan Campaign a Success," *The Mirror* 3: 9 (February 29, 1944); and "6th War Loan Drive," *The Mirror*, 4: 6 (November 20, 1944), Box 3, M&R Records, (VRHC); and Air Raids Pamphlet, M&R (1942), Box 12, M&R Records, (VRHC).

28 RNL (October 8, 1981).

Chapter Two

29 J. M. Golby, and A. W. Purdue, *The Making of the Modern Christmas* (B.T. Batsford Ltd: London, 1986) pp. 71-72; Leigh Eric Schimdt, *Consumer Rites: the Buying and Selling of American Holiday* (Princeton University Press,

Princeton, 1995); and Penne L. Restad, *Christmas in America: A History* (New York and Oxford: Oxford University Press, 1995).

30 Schimdt, pp. 164-165.

31 Ann Folks, "He wouldn't let women do window displays, but that was a year ago says Mr. Lewis," RTD (December 15, 1942); " Daily Throngs are tribute to M&R window displays," RTD (February 17, 1935); "Out of the 50 years it has been opened M&R workers join in tribute to 2 staff veterans," RTD (October 19, 1945); Lacy Jr., pp. 26-50; and *M&R Biography*, p. 14

32 Interview with Milton Burke (April 2001) and Allen Rhodes (April 2001); and Frank Walin, "Store Show Windows Gets Constant Changes," RTD (January 19, 1954).

33 "Punch and Judy Coming to Town," RTD (December 11, 1942); and "Santa stocks stores of city: windows gay," RNL (November 30, 1934).

34 Interview with Allen Rhodes, M&R employee. Mr. Rhodes worked on the M&R Train Windows.

35 David S. Hudson, "Window Man Plans Ahead," RTD (December 20, 1964).

36 "Stag shop will assist male buyers," RNL (November 30, 1945).

Chapter Three

37 I am not a liberty to discuss how Santa arrives in Richmond or where he resides during his stay. I promised Santa that I would not disclose this information.

38 Margaret Leonard, "Department store St. Nick with genuine whiskers is very real even in August," RTD (December 10, 1936).

39 Sandra Leigh Jett Ball's *Santa at Miller & Rhoads Painting* (1991) Francis & Art Hood Collection; and "Some of the Santas helpers who have presided in our M&R Wonderland," *The Mirror* (December 1953) Box 3, M&R Records, (VRHC).

40 Clifford Dowdy, "The World's Highest-Paid Santa Claus," *The Saturday Evening Post* (December 22, 1951), p.19; "Magic of Christmas at M&R," *This Week in Richmond* (December 24, c. 1960's), p. 15; and "Some of Santas Helpers who have Presided in our M&R Wonderland," *The Mirror* (December 1953) Box 3, M&R Records, (VRHC).

41 Interview with Claire Crostic (May 2001). Ms. Crostic visited with the M&R Santa as a child, and as a teenager, she worked at the store. Her own children grew up visiting the Real Santa Claus. Her memories helped supply the information for the following pages.

42 Letter to Art and Francis Hood from Hattie Garrison (November 25, 1985), Francis & Art Hood's Collection. Ms. Garrison was a M&R Snow Queen from 1959-1965; Dean Levi, "A Day with.... Santa Claus," RNL (December 21, 1972), p. 3; and Letter to Santa, from Mrs. Ralph D. Bradway, (December 6, 1979), Francis & Art Hood's Collection.

43 Interview with Allen Rhodes.

Chapter Four

44 Interview with Claire Crostic.

45 Interviews with Dan Rowe (May-June 2001) and Art Hood sipplied information about the M&R Santa Claus.

46 Roger Kintzel, "Santa Role Brings Fun," RNL (December 23, 1974); Jerry Lazarus, "Santa's Work Takes a Toll," RTD (December 16, 1976), p. D-1; Carol Mather, " By Golly, It's the Jolly Old Elf himself," *The Virginian-Pilot* (December 7, 1979), p. B-1; and Betsy Raper, "Holding onto Christmas," *Daily Press* (December 7, 1980), p. 4.

47 Interview with Art and Francis Hood (Fall 1996); Claire Crostic; Barbara Green's "Real Santa has been in Richmond nearly 50 Years," RNL (December 23, 1987); and Jack Kneece, "Stores Seek Fantasy, Sincerity in Santas," RNL (December 23, 1964).

48 Interview with Dan Rowe (May-June 2001); Letter to Santa, from Mrs. Phillips, (December 10, 1989); and Letter to Santa from Rosemarie and Randy, (December 1992), Francis & Art Hood's Collection.

49 Interview with Art and Francis Hood; Barbara Green, "Real Santa Has been in Richmond nearly 50 years," RNL (December 23, 1987), p. 16; Cindy McCurry, "CEO Claus Predicts Big Year for Wheels," Richmond Business Journal (Week of December 21 to 27, 1987), pp. 12-13; Letter to Santa from Ralph D. Bradway, (December 6, 1979), Charlottesville, Virginia, and Letter to Santa from Lynn Cohen, Virginia Beach, VA, (1983), Francis & Art Hood's Collection.

50 Interview with Claire Crostic.

51 Letter to the Editor of *Richmond-Lifestyle Magazine*, from Shirley Wiltshire, Francis & Art Hood's Collection.

52 Letter to Santa, from Mr. Russell O'Berry, Jr. and Letter to Mr. Robert J. Rieland, President of M&R from Mr. Russell O'Berry, Jr. (1984) Francis & Art Hood's Collection.

53 Old Dominion Chapter, National Railway Historical Society, Santa Train Display.

Chapter Five

54 I had many different sources about the Santa Train. Interviews with train passengers, Claire Crostic, Dan Rowe, Francis Hood and others. Newspaper articles: W. Rush Loving Jr. "Children," RTD (December 10, 1961); "Puzzled Frown, Wide Eyes and Contentment Highlight Gay Santa Claus Train Trip," RNL (December 6, 1958), p. 9; M&R Advertisement, RNL (November 20, 1958), p.31; "Santa Claus Trains to Mark 10th Year," RTD (December 1, 1967); "RF&P's Santa to Ride Again," RNL (December 4, 1963); "City Youngsters To Meet Santa Again In Ashland," RNL (December 5, 1962);

"Santa Specials Run Tomorrow," RNL (December 4, 1964); "Santa Trains Are Expecting 10,000 Riders," RNL (November 29, 1968); "Yule Train's First Run is Success," RTD (December 9, 1962); "St. Nick, Aide Supreme in Ride That's a Dream," RNL (December 11, 1961); Guy Friddell, "A Train Ride with St. Nick", RNL (December 12, 1960); "Meeting the Man," RNL (December 11, 1960); and "Santa Claus," *Mirror, 75th Anniversary Issue, 1885-1960* (December 1960).

55 " Derailed Santa Takes Party to M&R Tearoom," RTD (December 3, 1971); and Tyler Whitley, "Amtrak Derails Yuletide Train," RNL (November 5, 1971).

56 M&R Advertisement, RNL (December 5, 1923), p. 3; For Richmond during the 1920's see Tyler-McGraw, pp. 244-264; Ward, pp. 235-276; *Hill Directory for Richmond City, 1923*, pp. 1422-1431; and "The John T. Wilson Co., the Richmond Organization that Built The New Miller & Rhoads Grace Street Store," RTD (December 15, 1923), p. 20.

57 Jane Dierkes Waldron "Tea and History: Past Breeds Optimism at Tearoom," RNL (December 20, 1984), pp. 2 & 30; Interview with Milton Burke (Spring 1996 and May 2001), and "M&R Moves into its new Addition," RTD (November 30, 1923), p. 15.

58 Katherine Calos, "Experiencing Tea Room for Old Time's Sake," RNL (January 12, 1990); Calos, "Last Patrons Toast Tearoom with Rolls," RNL (July 17, 1991); and Betsy Raper "Tea Room Serves Up Goods Food, Goods Cheer," *Daily Press* (December 7, 1980), p. 6.

59 Interview with Dan Rowe and Lisa McDaniel Ramos.

60 Carol Mather, "By Golly, It's the Jolly Old Elf Himself."

61 Interview with Jody Weaver Wampler (June 2001); *The Mirror*, October-November 1958 (Volume 6 Number 8)

Box 10, M&R Records (VRHC), p. 3; Ted Shepherd, "Eddie Weaver," RNL (September 3, 1960); Frances Boushall, "Of Eddie Weaver and Pickled Peppers," RTD (September 12, 1948); "Weaver to Play in Silent Film Classic," RNL (March 20, 1982); "Eddie Weaver Makes Album," RTD (November 16, 1958); "Eddie Weaver To Do Show Over WRVA" RTD (April 28, 1950); Edith Lindeman, "Eddie Weaver to Quit Loew's," RTD (November 26, 1960); Jane Dierkes Waldron, "Past breed optimism at Tearoom," RNL (December 20, 1984), p. 29.

62 M&R advertisement, (November 25, 1985), Francis & Art Hood Collection.

63 "Fun for the Fawns," RNL (December 3, 1962); and Marguerite Davenport, "Shoppers on Piggy Back," RNL (November 30, 1956).

64 Interview with James Hurt (June 2001).

65 Letter to Hood from Roberta Carder, Director Volunteer Services, St. Jude Children's Research Hospital (January 11, 1984), Art Hood sent Santa posters to all the children and in 1987, Hood sent teddy bears and received a thank-you note from St. Judes Director of Communications (December 14, 1987), Francis & Art Hood Collection. Capital visits: Governor John N. Dalton (*The Mirror* 1953); Governor Charles S. Robb (December 3, 1982); Governor Lawrence Douglas Wilder (December 31, 1991), Francis & Art Hood Collection. Outside visits: "Santa Visits Riverside Convalescent Center in Mathews," *Daily-Press* (November 25, 1992), p. 10; "Santa brunch a Giving Extravaganza," *The Winds of Hermitage* (January 1993), Santa visits Hermitage Country Club and the brunches have more than 750 people attend, Francis & Art Hood Collection.

Chapter Six

66 Milton Burke transports the M&R Santa Claus every year to the Virginia Home. Together they hand out presents to each resident. Mr. Burke works throughout the year collecting donations to fund this wonderful tradition. If you would like to contribute, please send your donation to: Milton Burke, 100 N. Belmont Ave., Richmond, VA 23221. Thank you!

67 Letter to Santa, from Mrs. N. L. Armistead, Jr. (1964), Francis & Art Hood's Collection.

68 "Santa Claus Pays Visit to Orphans," RNL (December 14, 1934), p. 11.

69 Letter to Robert Hardy, VP of Sales Promotions, from Thelma J. Parsons (November 29, 1986), Francis & Art Hood's Collection.

70 Stan Beason, "Ho! Ho! Ho! and interview with the Jolly Old Elf," *The Carolina Progress* (December 25, 1991), p. 1-2.

Chapter Seven

71 Letter from Daniel D. Bramos (December 19, 1980), Francis & Art Hood Collection.

72 John Stockley, President, M&R Court Transcript (September 15, 1989), Bankruptcy File 8, M&R Bankruptcy Records; and Bankruptcy File 19, M&R Bankruptcy Records.

73 Letter to Santa, from Mrs. Phillips (December 10, 1989), and Letter to Santa, from Dean and Cam, Francis & Art Hood's Collection Ann Holiday; "Santa will be back at M&R," RNL (August 12, 1989) p. 34; Mike Allen, "Line to Santa Binds Families in Ritual of Joy," RTD (November 1989), p. 1; and Bonnie V. Winston, "Santa May be Buyout Casualty," *Northern Virginian Pilot, Ledger Star* (October 1, 1989) p. A2.

74 Winston, "Santa may be buyout casualty."

75 Randy Hallman, "On the Block, Auctioneers Hammer Could Fall on Santas Chair," RNL (March 15, 1990), Francis & Art Hood Collection. Interview with Christina S. Risatti, Executive Director, Downtown Presents (March 15, 2001). Downtown Presents is a nonprofit business founded in 1985. Downtown Presents pamphlet 2001 events states their mission: "Our mission is to unite metropolitan area through community events and festivals that promote downtown Richmond, Virginia"; Ann Holiday, "Santa Claus is coming to downtown M&R," RNL (November 12, 1991).

Bibliography

Collections

Miller & Rhoads Records. Valentine Richmond History Center, Richmond, Virginia. (VRHC).

Francis & Art Hood Collection.

Miller & Rhoads Bankruptcy Court Records. Author's Collection. (M&R Bankruptcy Records).

Richmond Times Dispatch Research Archives

Articles

"Stores." *The New York Times Magazine*, section 6 (April 6, 1997) pp. 45-86.

Berry, Leonard L., "The New Consumer," in Ronald W. Stampfl and Elizabeth Hirschman, eds., *Competitive Structure in Retail Markets: The Department Store Perspective* (Chicago, Illinois, American Marketing Association, 1980) p. 1-11.

Cohen, Lizabeth, "From Town Center to Shopping Center: The Reconfiguration of Community Marketplaces in Postwar America." in *American Historical Review*, (October 1996), pp. 1050-1081.

Gutman, Herbert G., "Work, Culture, and Society in Industrializing America, 1815-

1919." *American Historical Review*, 78:3, (June 1973) pp. 531-588.

Murphy, Thomas P., "Race-Base Accounting: Assigning the Costs and Benefits of a Racially Motivated Annexation." *Urban Affairs Quarterly*, 14:2, (December 1978) pp. 169-194.

Silver, Christopher, "The Ordeal of City Planning in Postwar Richmond, Virginia: A Quest for Greatness." *Journal of Urban History*, 10: 1, p. 33-60.

Wilentz, Sean, "Artisan Republican Festivals and the Rise of Class conflict in New York City, 1788-1837" *Working Class America: Essays on Labor, Community and American Society*, ed. Michael H. Frisch and Daniel J. Walkowitz, (Urbana, University of Illinois Press, 1983) pp. 37-77.

Books

Abelson, Elaine S. *When Ladies Go-A-Thieving: Middle Class Shoplifters in the Victorian Department Store*. (New York and Oxford, Oxford University Press, 1989).

Barmash, Isadore. *More Than They Bargained For: The Rise and Fall of Korvettes*. (Lebhar-

Friedman Books/Chain Store Publishing Corp, 1981).

Benson, Susan Porter. *Counter Cultures: Saleswomen, Managers, and Customers in American Department Stores, 1890-1940.* (Urbana and Chicago, University of Illinois Press, 1986).

Bluestone, Barry, Patricia Hanna, Sarah Kuhn, and Laura Moore, *The Retail Revolution: Market Transformation, Investment, and Labor in the Modern Department Store.* (Boston, Auburn House Publication Company, 1981).

Blumin, Stuart. *The Emergence of the Middle Class: Social Experience in the American City, 1760-1900.* (Cambridge, Cambridge University Press, 1989).

Bryant, Keith L. Jr. and Henry C. Dethloff, *A History of American Business.* (Englewood Cliffs, New Jersey, Prentice-Hall, Inc, 1990).

Covington, Howard E. Jr. *Belk: A Century of Retail Leadership.* (Chapel Hill and London, The University of North Carolina Press, 1988).

Cowan, Ruth Schwartz. *More Work For Mothers: The Ironies of Household Technology from the Open Hearth to the Microwave.* (New York, Basic Books, Inc., 1983).

Dabney, Virginius. *Richmond: The Story of a City.* (University of Virginia, Charlottesville, 1990).

Dumenil, Lynn. *Modern Temper: American Culture and Society in the 1920's.* (New York, Hill and Wang, 1995).

Evans, Sara M. *Born for Liberty: A History of Women in America.* (New York, The Free Press, 1989).

Guilford, Martha G. ed. *From Founders to Grandsons: The Story of Woodward &*

Lothrop. (Washington, D. C., Rufus H. Barby Printing Company, 1955).

Gutman, Max. *The Elder-Beerman Stores Corporation: A Tradition of Success.* (New York, Newcomen Society of United States, 1984).

Harvey, Brett. *The Fifties: A Women's Oral History.* (New York, HarperPernnial, 1993).

Lancaster, William. *The Department Store: A Social History.* (London and New York, Leicester University Press, 1995).

Leach, William. *Land of Desire: Merchants, Power, and the Rise of a New American Culture.* (New York, Vintage Books, 1994).

Lebhar, Godfrey. *Chain Stores in America, 1859-1962.* (Colonial Press Inc, Clinton Mass, 1963).

Levine, Lawrence W. *Highbrow Lowbrow: The Emergence of Cultural Hierarchy in America.* (Cambridge, MA, Harvard University Press, 1988).

Marchand, Roland. *Advertising the American Dream: Making Way for Modernity, 1920-1940.* (Berkeley, University of California Press, 1985).

McNair, Malcolm P. and Eleanor G. May, *The American Department Store 1920-1960: A Performance Analysis Based on the Harvard Reports.* (Graduate School of Business, Harvard University, 1963).

Miller, Michael Barry. *The Bon Marche: Bourgeois Culture and the Department Store.* (Princeton, N.J., Princeton University Press, 1981).

Reekie, Gail. *Temptations: Sex, Selling, and the Department Store.* (Sydney: Allen & Unwin, 1993)

Rosenberg, Joseph. *Sangers' Pioneer Texas Merchants*. (Austin, Texas, Texas State Historical Association, 1978).

Sanford, James K. editor, *A Century of Commerce, 1867-1967*. (Richmond Chamber of Commerce, Richmond, Virginia, 1967).

Slater, Don. *Consumer Culture & Modernity*. (Polity Press, Cambridge, 1997).

Stampfl, Ronald W. and Elizabeth Hirschman's. *Competitive Structure in Retail Markets: The Department Store Perspective*. (Chicago, Illinois, American Marketing Association, 1980).

Sussman, Warren, *Culture as History: The Transformation of American Society in the Twentieth Century*. (New York, Pantheon Books, 1984).

Tedlow, Richard S. *New and Improved: The Story of Mass Marketing in America*. (New York, Basic Books, 1990).

Tyler-McGraw, Marie. *At The Falls, Richmond, Virginia, & Its People*. (Chapel Hill & London, The University of North Carolina Press, 1994).

Ward, Harry Ward. *Richmond, An Illustrated History*. (Northridge, CA, Windsor Publications, 1985).